Riveting Reads

A World of Books in Translation

JOY COURT
AND
DANIEL HAHN

SERIES EDITOR: GEOFF DUBBER

SLA
School Library Association

Dedication: Anthea Bell O.B.E.

This edition of *Riveting Reads* features the work of dozens of talented translators, but among them all one is unquestionably supreme. Over a fifty-year career her work has been more astonishingly versatile, and more prolific, and brought more sheer delight to readers than any other translator we can think of. Indeed, she has come to be thought of – by readers, publishers and her peers alike – as a kind of figurehead for the translation of children's books. Her friends and colleagues were delighted to celebrate her eightieth birthday with her in Cambridge a few months ago, and we are proud to dedicate this publication to her now, with affection and the greatest admiration. This edition of *Riveting Reads* is for Anthea.

Acknowledgments

The authors wish to thank all those people who took a kind interest in this project and provided their thoughts and recommendations. Particularly Kevin Crossley-Holland, whose initial idea it was and who has written such an erudite Introduction, and Wendy Cooling, whose idea it was to include the entertaining vignettes from the great and good. With thanks to the great and good: David Almond, Michael Rosen, Klaus Flugge, Zoë Adams, Jane Winterbotham, Julia Eccleshare, John Newman, Ann Harding, Gill Evans, Gillian Lathey, Laura Watkinson, Sarah Ardizzone, Meg Rosoff, Axel Scheffler, Cornelia Funke, Adam Freudenheim, Zoe Toft, Emily Malone, Siân Williams, Alexandra Strick, Deborah Hallford, Emma Langley, Alex Valente, Mara Faye Lethem and Tricia Adams.

The series editor would like to thank Charlotte Weatherley who expressed an interest in this publication from its inception and SLA Board member Margaret Pemberton, both of whom kindly looked over and commented on the text for us.

Published by:
School Library Association
1 Pine Court, Kembrey Park
Swindon SN2 8AD
Tel: 01793 530166 Fax: 01793 481182
Email: publications@sla.org.uk
Web: www.sla.org.uk

Registered Charity No: 313660
Charity Registered in Scotland No: SC039453

© School Library Association 2017
All rights reserved.
ISBN 978-1-911222-00-2

Printed by Holywell Press, Oxford

Riveting **Reads:** A World of Books in Translation

Contents

Introduction by Kevin Crossley-Holland 4

Other Voices 6

A Note from the Editors 8

A World of Books in Translation

    Under 8 9

    Where it all began... myths, legends, fairy tales and fables 18

    8 to 12 21

    12 to 14 41

    14+ 49

Beyond this... 56

Index of Authors 58

Index of Titles 59

Index of Translators 60

Series editor's note: The ISBN numbers given in this publication are indicative of currently available titles; other editions and formats may be available.

Riveting **Reads:** A World of Books in Translation

Introduction

Suppose the absurd! Suppose Her Majesty's Government were to propose legislation banning the translation into English of foreign children's books.

What would happen? Well, of course there would be an outcry, a howl of disbelief from all quarters political, commercial and cultural. And yet the truth is that, until the last few years, and with the exception of a handful of classics, dismally few foreign children's books have been translated into English. Indeed, only a laughably small percentage of all trade books are translations.

Why this should be so is a thorny question with no single answer. Partly, it's a lack of curiosity and partly a matter of profit margins, but there's also a sense that it's just much easier to publish more books by native English-speaking authors, thank you very much, than to search out foreign ones, and then to find expert translators – not so very difficult with European translators, but often problematic when it comes to the Middle and Far East, Africa...

Nonetheless, one can't think of the story of British children's books without including a fair number of translations (a mass of folk-tales among them) and I imagine that, like me, most school librarians will have heard and read some books as children without having had the least idea that they were actually translations. In my case, it was *Fattypuffs and Thinifers* and *Swiss Family Robinson* and Wilhelm and Jacob Grimm, while my mother's favourite was *Struwwelpeter* because of its comic (but not so comic) horrors and its rectitude.

In providing us with an authoritative assessment of children's books translated into English (both the originals and their translations), this Riveting Reads breaks completely new ground and is likely to mark a turning-point in the awareness of translated children's books. And it could scarcely be more timely in so far as more organisations, universities and publishers are supporting translation (as, for instance, The Children's Bookshow, the British Centre for Literary Translation at the University of East Anglia and Pushkin Children's Books have long since done), not only because the best foreign novels and picture books are quite outstanding but also because they're the cornerstone of crucial cultural exchange and are of huge educational value; all the more so at a time when individuals and families from so many different countries and cultures are working and settling in the United Kingdom.

With this recognition has come a deepening awareness of just how difficult translation actually is. I've regularly seen this at firsthand while leading workshops for adults and children, and corresponding with my own meticulous translators; and I've experienced it while trying to translate short pieces from French and Norwegian, as well as struggling for four years during my twenties with the epic Anglo-Saxon poem *Beowulf*. Margaret Atwood is right: 'The choices that bedevil the writer bedevil the translator ten times over.'

How thrilling it is to step as a young reader into a world at once familiar and unfamiliar – just the same yet strangely different. But this spell can be so quickly broken by a wrong word. Maintaining suspension of disbelief: this is the tightrope that translators have to walk, and it's all the more challenging when their author is in love with language, and writes playfully and stylishly, however simple the words.

It should now follow that we have come quite a way from the time when translators were treated as secondary, and relatively insignificant. But no, we haven't. On title pages, their names are customarily printed in small type, and in a few cases they're omitted altogether. This, frankly, is a disgrace, and the perpetrators should be named and shamed.

Like many of you, and in particular our two very distinguished editors, I've long felt the need for a publication such as this. Since calling on the School Library Association to espouse it just a couple of years ago, while speaking at the Marsh Awards, I've become aware of being part of a groundswell advocating more translation – more translation casting its net far and wide while affirming (since some seem to doubt it!) that British and European cultures are and always have been indivisible.

So here it is – an important and influential stepping-stone. It will help you as you help young readers to fulfil what they are: world citizens.

Kevin Crossley-Holland
Author and President of the School Library Association

Other Voices

Books in translation help us all to reach beyond our own language and culture. As a writer, if I hadn't read Márquez, I could not have written *Skellig*. Without *Pippi Longstocking*, there would be no *My Dad's a Birdman*. Without books in translation, my life and world would be diminished.

—David Almond, author

Encountering an 'Oma' in one of my early books at primary school made me realise, perhaps for the first time, that not everyone in the world speaks English. Oma was like my nan, but she was… Oma. She sent me on a fascinating journey of exploration into other languages and cultures, a journey that readers everywhere can enjoy. Thanks, Oma!

—Laura Watkinson, translator

Translation provides children with invaluable access to the people, places and events which form our worlds. Through translated texts, children are able to discover the voices of their international peers, to engage with their stories, and to weave these narratives into their understanding of the world around them.

—Zoë Adams, cultural exchange officer, English-Speaking Union

I have enjoyed a ten-year bookselling relationship with Gallions PS which provides P4C training to teachers across the south-east. Picture books are a key resource for introducing an enquiry and promoting discussion and facilitative learning. Over time a number of key texts have been picture books in translation. They are very often books which do not shy away from dealing with complex and difficult issues and they can be challenging and I never tire of putting them into people's hands and awaiting their reactions.

—John Newman, bookseller

Storytime in an Islington infants' school in the 1980s. Glorious memories of taking children into the surreal world of Peter Bichsel's *Stories for Children*; to 1920s Berlin (Kästner's *Emil and the Detectives*), or on a visual journey with the monkey god Hanuman. Difference fascinates children and, as Astrid Lindgren put it: 'their imagination continues to build where the translator can go no further.'
—Gillian Lathey, children's literature scholar

I happen to believe that children have a right to view the planet they inhabit from the perspective of writers and illustrators the world over. And to share – with children whose countries they can only dream of visiting – in an international territory of the imagination. When I visit schools, I often refer to two books I've had the privilege of translating: *The Rights of the Reader* by Daniel Pennac, illustrated by Quentin Blake, which is about the power of stories; and *I Have the Right to Be a Child* by Alain Serres, illustrated by Aurélia Fronty, which explores UNESCO's Convention of the Rights of the Child. Together, we talk about the right to read books in translation.
—Sarah Ardizzone, translator

" Translated children's literature can broaden our horizons, helping to break down the barriers of geography, language and race, and build bridges between nations. We can help develop tolerance and understanding of other peoples' beliefs and cultures, by enabling young audiences to access, explore and enjoy books from other countries. Now, more than ever, Britain must not become culturally insular, so we must encourage more books published from different languages. There is a wonderful array of rich tradition and culture in children's literature from around the world that needs to be experienced by UK readers.
—Deborah Hallford, Outside In World "

A Note from the Editors

'Books in translation' can sound like a rather niche interest, can't it? But try thinking about it another way: well over ninety percent of the world's population aren't first-language speakers of English, so when we're talking about translated books, that is what we're covering. 'Books in translation' means all the output of continental Europe, most of Africa, all of Latin America and most of Asia. Some niche! So the books we have chosen for this guide are as varied as you'd expect, in genre and style and voice and age and, well, every other category – the only things they have in common are that they once began life in another language and that they are very, very good. (It's true that we don't translate enough children's books in the UK, given how much there is to choose from, but it does mean publishers set the bar for translated books that much higher!) We've included the great international classics that many of us will have grown up with; right up to the new books that we think will be the international classics of the future. So we hope you and your readers find some old favourites, but we hope you'll discover some new ones, too.

Joy Court and Daniel Hahn

How to Use This Volume

The selected books are arranged in categories relating closely to the usual review sections in *The School Librarian* and arranged alphabetically by author within those sections. An approximate age level is given but we all know this can be no substitute for knowing the reader for whom you are recommending the book. It was a sad fact that when we came to compiling the list that all too many favourite titles had gone out of print; but the books chosen for this guide were all available at the time of writing, and are listed by their most recent edition.

Under 8

ALEMAGNA, BEATRICE

Translated from the Italian by Claudia Zoe Bedrick

The Marvellous Fluffy Squishy Itty Bitty

Thames & Hudson, 2015   ISBN: 9780500650493

One morning, Eddie wakes up and hears her little sister say these words: birthday—mama—present—fluffy—little—squishy. Worried that her sister will find one before she does, Eddie runs off on a hunt. But where should she begin? Eddie's search – magical and entirely her own – leads her just where she needs to go. Beatrice Alemagna's long list of accolades includes the Premio Andersen Award, a Bologna Ragazzi Mention, five White Ravens Awards and three Baobab Prizes for the most innovative books for children. In this delightful example of her work she perfectly captures a child's innocent view of the world and the wonders it contains. **4+**

BARROUX

Translated from the French by Sarah Ardizzone

Mr Leon's Paris

Phoenix Yard, 2012   ISBN: 9781907912085

Who better to give you a tour of the delights of Paris than Mr Leon, a veteran Parisian taxi driver, as we accompany him on his shift with his very varied array of passengers? And who better to tell Mr Leon's story than book artist *extraordinaire* Barroux, whose inimitable pictures conjure up his own version of the city in such a suggestive and stylish fashion? And as if that wasn't enough, Barroux's original playful text has been recreated by Sarah Ardizzone, one of the best translators in the business. Get ready for an unforgettable ride! **4+**

BAUER, JUTTA

Translated from the German. No translator attributed.

Grandpa's Guardian Angel

Walker, 2015   ISBN: 9781406306033

'Grandpa always loved telling stories,' it begins. We watch him tell stories of how lucky he had been as a fearless young boy, always getting himself into trouble, but with a guardian angel always ready to get him out of it in the nick of time. But Grandpa hadn't realised how dangerous things really were, until one day his friend Joseph, who wore a yellow star, disappeared… Yes, there were tough times, says Grandpa, but all in all it was a good life, and yes, that guardian angel stayed there with him all the way. A really touching and thought-provoking story from one of Germany's great contemporary illustrator-authors. **4+**

BEHRANGI, SAMAD
Translated from the Persian by Azita Rassi. Illustrated by Farshid Mesghali

The Little Black Fish

Tiny Owl Publishing, 2015 ISBN: 9781910328002

Gorgeously illustrated in this Tiny Owl edition by Farshid Mesghali, the first ever Asian winner of the Hans Christian Andersen Award, *The Little Black Fish* has been called Iran's most famous children's book of all time. As with most animal stories it can certainly be read as an allegory and its political reading ensured that it was banned in pre-revolution Iran. You can see why the story of the little fish who defies convention (and his Mother!) swim away from the small section of the stream which confines their lives on a quest to find out 'if the stream goes on and on, or whether it comes to an end.' Throughout his journey he meets other creatures who also believe that there is nowhere else beyond their own limited environment and that their way of life and their view of the world is the only way to be. **5+**

BLAKE, STÉPHANIE
Translated from the French by Linda Burgess

Poo Bum

Gecko Press, 2013 ISBN: 9781877467974

Stéphanie Blake has written and illustrated dozens of popular French children's books renowned for their insight into the anarchic world of childhood. This is perhaps the best known and loved and introduces us to Simon, a little rabbit who could only say one thing! The little rabbit is loved by his family, even though whenever they ask him a question, he answers very rudely as you might guess from the title. One day, he meets a hungry wolf. Will the little rabbit learn his lesson once and for all? This is genuinely funny with bold and incredibly expressive illustrations which instantly attract the eye. You can find more laughs with Simon in **Stupid Baby** (9781877579318) and **A Deal's a Deal** (9781877579837). **2+**

BRUNA, DICK
Translated from the Dutch by Tony Mitton

Miffy

Simon & Schuster, 2014 ISBN: 9781471120787

Dick Bruna's books have had the same signature format for over 60 years. They are compact, square, perfectly sized for small hands and consist of 12 spreads, with the distinctive primary coloured drawings on the right and four lines of (rhyming) text on the left. Here Mr and Mrs Bunny decide to have a baby, and they call her Miffy. This little rabbit becomes Dick Bruna's best known and most universally popular character, featuring in more than 30 books. She is uncomplicated and innocent, has a positive attitude and is always open to new experiences. Award-winning UK poet, Tony Mitton, has created new translations for the classic Miffy stories that are true to the books' original warm and friendly voice, and yet are contemporary and appealing to a modern young audience. **2+**

CHEN, CHIH-YUAN
Translated from the Chinese by Kane Miller

Guji-Guji

Gecko Press, 2009 ISBN: 9781877467431

Chih-Yuan Chen is an award-winning illustrator and writer from Taiwan, and the beautiful muted tones of the watercolour and ink illustrations really add to the delights of this story about a befuddled 'crocoduck' who comes to appreciate families and differences. It also comes with the added bonus of a positive message about reading. When an egg rolls into Mother Duck's clutch, she doesn't notice because she's reading, and she quite happily accepts it as hers; it becomes part of her duck family, doing everything that ducks do, including having a bedtime story! But when Guji-Guji meets three crocodiles who closely resemble him, he has to consider where his loyalties lie when they try to persuade him to bring his duck family along for them to eat. **3+**

ĆOPIĆ, BRANKO

Translated from the Serbo-Croatian by S.D. Curtis. Illustrated by Sanja Rešček

Hedgehog's Home

Istros Books, 2011   ISBN: 9781908236029

First published in Yugoslavia in 1951, this was a narrative poem that could be recited by almost every Yugoslav adult and child since first written by one of the Balkans' best known authors. It survived the wars to become part of the culture of the newly formed republics of the early 1990s and the book still remains on the Croatian school curriculum. Hedgemond is a very determined and stubborn little Hedgehog who loves his home deep in the forest and is determined to get back to it as quickly as possible, much to the puzzlement of other animals who follow him as they think he must have treasure to protect. **4+**

DE BEER, HANS

Translated from the Dutch by Rosemary Lanning

Little Polar Bear

NorthSouth Books, 2016   ISBN: 9780735842649

Hans de Beer's popular Little Polar Bear series, which began with this title, is a gentle introduction to the concepts of friendship, family, courage, nature, and environmentalism. Lars wakes up to find that the ice on which he was sleeping is floating south. He reaches a tropical land with no snow or ice but with amazing new colours! Though there is much to see and do, Lars becomes homesick. His new friends arrange to get Lars back home, where he is happily reunited with his anxious parents. The beautiful watercolour illustrations of the polar landscape and the endearing bear are an important part of the enduring appeal of this Dutch classic. **3+**

DE BRUNHOFF, JEAN

Translated from the French by Olive Jones

The Story of Babar

Egmont, 2008   ISBN: 9781405238182

In this first volume in the famous series of elegant large-format picture books, we meet Babar the little elephant in the Great Forest. After his mother is killed by a hunter, young Babar runs away to the city and is adopted by a rich old lady (who gives him nice clothes to wear, including his now immediately recognizable green suit). By the end of the book he has returned to the forest and been elected King of the Elephants, with bride-to-be Celeste as his Queen. In later stories, Babar travels the world, builds a city and meets Father Christmas. Babar has become a major international brand today, but this book is where it all started. **4+**

ERLBRUCH, WOLF

Translated from the German by Catherine Chidgey

Duck, Death and the Tulip

Gecko Press, 2008   ISBN: 9781877467141

Considered to be the award-winning German author's masterpiece, this is beautiful, gentle and deeply affecting. Many would consider the subject of death as unsuitable for young children but the way this is tackled in such an elegant and matter of fact way, without a shred of sentimentality and engaging light humour makes this a very useful book to share when children inevitably ask questions as they all do. **5+**

> This is the finest meditation on death I've ever read. Not the finest for children, the finest ever. Tender, unflinching and true, it resonates for all ages on the most difficult subject of all. We hear a great deal about masterpieces of literature. *Duck, Death and the Tulip* is the real thing.
>
> —Meg Rosoff, author

GUETTIER, BÉNÉDICTE

Translated from the French by Lizzie Kelly

The Dad with 10 Children

Scribblers, 2014   ISBN: 9781909645844

Dads are relatively rare creatures in picture books and in this, the first of a zany series, from this French author specialising in books for the early years, we meet a careworn single parent. Every day, the dad who had 10 children counted 10 little t-shirts, 10 cups on the table, 10 bowls of spaghetti and 10 goodnight kisses… until one day he finally needed a rest! Leaving his 10 children with Grandma, he set off for a break from counting. But after just 10 peaceful days and 10 quiet nights, he discovers that something is definitely missing and a nautical reunion follows. The black edged boldly coloured illustrations immediately attract the attention of young audiences. **2+**

HOFFMANN, HEINRICH

Translated from the German by Alexander Platt

Struwwelpeter

Dover Children's Classics   ISBN: 9780486284699

This collection of illustrated rhyming cautionary tales is deliciously disturbing and wickedly funny. With great relish it tells the stories of a boy who sucks his thumbs (they get cut off), a girl who plays with matches (and burns to death), the aptly named Bad Frederick (who gets bitten by a dog), and many more, all of them badly-behaved children whose sticky ends are exaggerated in their gruesomeness but presented to us as entirely deserved. Moralising tales of this kind have long gone out of fashion, but even 170 years on this unique collection seems as energetic as it's ever been. Among many other successors, it inspired the verses Roald Dahl included for each of the revolting children in *Charlie and the Chocolate Factory*. **4+**

HOLZWARTH, WERNER

Translated from the German. No translator attributed. Illustrated by Wolf Erlbruch

The Story of the Little Mole Who Knew It Was None of His Business

Pavilion Books, 1994   ISBN: 9781856021012

Nothing less than a scatological masterpiece and an international success since its first publication in 1989, this is also a book that really established the reputation of Wolf Erlbruch for his outstandingly expressive illustrations. Little Mole's body language changes in every phase of the story: surprised, hungry, interested, analytical, scared, resigned and finally satisfied in the end as he solves the mystery of who left something unpleasant on his head on one bright and sunny morning. All those not easily offended will be amused and small children will be entranced by the opportunity to discuss one of their favourite obsessions. **3+**

JANOSCH

Translated from the German by Anthea Bell

The Trip to Panama

Beltz, 2015   ISBN: 9783407760258

Janosch is one of Germany's best-known artists and children's book authors. He has published over one hundred books for children translated into over thirty languages. His most famous and popular character is the Tigerente. Literally a tiger duck it is a little wooden toy duck on wheels, striped black on yellow, which is pulled around on a string by various characters in Janosch's books. Without a single line of dialogue, it has become by far the most popular figure ever created by the author and features in this charming story about learning to appreciate what you have. One day, a wonderful-smelling crate floats past their riverside home, with the word PANAMA written on it. Little bear and little tiger decide that Panama must be the land of their dreams, and set off on a quest to find it. **4+**

KAZEMI, NAHID

Translated from the Persian by Azita Rassi

The Orange House

Tiny Owl, 2016   ISBN: 9781910328118

From a new publisher dedicated to global children's literature, this subtle story of belonging, friendship and intergenerational respect is truly beautiful. The Persian author illustrator used to hand-make and paint her own books as a child and this tactile feel is preserved in the imagery of this tale of an old house left behind by all the new tall skyscrapers. Yet it shows how we can incorporate and remain sympathetic to our cultural heritage whilst keeping up with the needs of a fast-paced and growing world. **4+**

KÖNNECKE, OLE

Translated from the German by Catherine Chidgey

Anton Can Do Magic

Gecko Press, 2010   ISBN: 9781877467370

What is wonderful about this book from a prize-winning German author and illustrator is that, although the reader can see what 'really' happens, the characters' perception that Anton can do magic is never challenged! It's a lovely representation of the interplay between fantasy and reality that is such an important part of child development. The expressive illustrations are all in warm red and yellow tones, and the minimal text manages to convey an excellent story and sense of humour. **You Can Do It Bert** (2014, 9781927271032) is another triumph that will encourage all young children to rise to a challenge. **3+**

LERAY, MARJOLAINE
Translated from the French by Sarah Ardizzone
April the Red Goldfish
Phoenix Yard Books, 2014   ISBN: 9781907912405

Goldfish are often seen as rather boring pets but after reading this surreal, zany book you will never be able to look at them in the same light again. Full of teen angst, existential ponderings and a true spirit of rebellion, April is quite a character. Darkly funny and with the characteristic red palette and scribbly images and texts that made this author's version of the traditional Red Riding Hood tale so popular (*Little Red Hood*), this is not to be missed. **7+**

MARTINS, ISABEL MINHÓS
Translated from the Portuguese by Daniel Hahn. Illustrated by Bernardo Carvalho
Don't Cross the Line!
Gecko Press, 2016   ISBN: 9781776570744

A slapstick postmodern meta-fictional tale, from a Portuguese author and illustrator duo, that is also a profound statement about dictatorship and peaceful revolution. The guard always follows the general's orders without question. This time, the order is that no one must cross the line. The right-hand page of this book must be kept blank for the general's sole use. As the crowd builds up on the border, the guard is under pressure. But people power and the age-old request to collect a stray ball triumph in the end. It is those eight blank pages that have a power beyond words: children see an empty space and want to play in it, a teenager will rebel against anything forbidden and adults see the injustice of the overcrowding they are suffering. The 60+ playful, vividly drawn, unique characters not only reveal their own little stories, they tell a true tale for our times. **5+**

NILSSON, ULF
Translated from the Swedish by Julia Marshall. Illustrated by Eva Eriksson
When We Were Alone in the World
Gecko Press, 2010   ISBN: 9781877467349

An example of the wonderful partnership of two Astrid Lindgren Prize winners, this is an extraordinarily warm and funny book about a big brother's courage and inventiveness when he discovers his parents have been run over by a truck – or have they? Maybe his newly acquired telling-the-time skills are actually at fault! The caring sibling relationship is beautifully depicted in the subtle, evocative, expressive images and the dry laconic humour of the text is a real paean to a child's imagination and resourcefulness. Nilsson really has an astonishing facility for inhabiting the child's point of view. **3+**

OHMURA, TOMOKO
Translated from the Japanese by Cathy Hirano
Line Up, Please!
Gecko Press, 2014   ISBN: 9781877579981

This award-winning author from Japan has created the perfect book about queuing. Just what are all these 50 animals waiting in line for? As we count down, the size of the animal increases and so do their humorous grumbles. Number 4 is a Hippopotamus who 'can't wait another second' and number 3 a Rhinoceros who claims 'I'm going to charge'. The double page gatefold at the end reveals a wonderful climax and the bold colourful illustrations will keep younger children engrossed in identifying the animals; and older children will enjoy the witty repartee and the mystery. **3+**

PFISTER, MARCUS

Translated from the German by J. Alison James

The Rainbow Fish

NorthSouth, 2007   ISBN: 9780735820845

Rainbow Fish is the most beautiful fish in the sea, but he won't play with the other fish, and won't let them have any of his gorgeous shiny scales, even though he has lots and lots. So he's lonely, and it's his own fault! But will he learn his lesson? This hugely popular story has a nice 'it's good to share' moral built in, and Rainbow Fish's glittering scales are indeed lovely, with small patterned foil panels inset in every page, making this popular book a shiny visual treat. (Rainbow Fish is available in a range of formats including board books, bath books, lift-the-flap books, games and even an interactive, computer storybook. The picture book sequels include *Rainbow Fish and His Friends: Hidden Treasures*; *Rainbow Fish to the Rescue* and *Rainbow Fish and the Big Blue Whale*.) **3+**

ROY, SANDRINE DUMAS

Translated from the French by Sarah Ardizzone. Illustrated by Emmanuelle Houssais

Hot Air

Phoenix Yard, 2013   ISBN: 9781907912221

How on earth to talk to young children about global warming and environmental politics? Well, this French picture-book may just be the answer. It's energetic, engaging and colourful, filled with lively, noisy animals in exuberant collage illustrations, but the message in it is serious and clear throughout: we're in a bad way, and something must be done. *Hot Air* will inform children, but also encourage and empower them to find out more. It even ends with a question: 'anyone out there got any bright ideas?' **4+**

STARK, ULF

Translated from the Swedish by Julia Marshall. Illustrated by Anna Höglund

Can You Whistle, Johanna?

Gecko Press, 2009   ISBN: 9780958259859

Winner of the Deutscher Jugendliteraturpreis (German Youth Literature Prize) in 1994, this Swedish classic tells how Ulf suggests to his friend Berra that he might find himself a grandfather by visiting the local retirement home and choosing one of the residents there. This he does with often delightful consequences for them all. A poignant story that does not shirk the fact that old people inevitably die, it is also very funny and is said to be Ulf Stark's own favourite title. **4+**

STRID, JAKOB MARTIN

Translated from the Danish by Anna McQuinn

Little Frog

Alanna Books, 2009   ISBN: 9780955199868

The Danish political cartoonist famous for his comic strip alter ego *Strid* won a children's publishing picture book competition with *Little Frog* in 2005, and this book then won the BØFA Cultural Honorary Award, and Strid went on to create many more successful picture books. What makes this one so special? Everyone with children will recognise the naughty little frog. Children will be relieved at the idea that there might be someone naughtier than them and every naughty child needs to know that discipline does not mean withdrawal of love. In a beautifully simple way it captures the urge for exploration and independence, the inevitable frustration and, most importantly, the need for acceptance that every 'frog' seeks. It even shows that children who have had problems in childhood can become successful in later life. **3+**

TAGHDIS, SUSAN

Translated from the Persian by Azita Rassi. Illustrated by Ali Mafakheri

The Snowman and the Sun

Tiny Owl, 2015   ISBN: 9781910328101

What happens to a snowman when the sun comes out? He melts, of course. And then he turns into water, evaporates, returns to the sky and falls again as rain or, as in this case, snow. This modern-day fable, from an Iranian author and illustrator partnership, can make children think about how our attachments to people and things live on even though they change and sometimes disappear and can also be an excellent way to introduce the water cycle. The child-like artwork on a graph-paper background has lovely humorous touches, such as the bumble bee riding a bicycle. **3+**

TELLEGEN, TOON

Translated from the Dutch by Bill Nagelkerke. Illustrated by Marc Boutavant

The Day No One Was Angry

Gecko Press, 2016   ISBN: 9781927271605

Twelve stunningly illustrated, poetic, and funny stories about grumpy animals from an internationally acclaimed Dutch writer and a hugely popular French illustrator. Winner of the Zilveren Penseel in 2015, these stories are funny and wry, but also offer a gently profound reflection of the nature of human emotions. **6+**

> One of my favourite books in translation is *The Day No One Was Angry*. Feeling angry – with or without reason – a feeling familiar to all of us, children as well as grown-ups. The wonderful Dutch writer Toon Tellegen explores all this in a series of touching short stories set in his crazy animal world of aardvarks, ants, hippos, squirrels, beetles and rhinos (and many more). I had the honour to illustrate one of his collections for a French publisher once, but I must admit that I much prefer what Marc Boutavant did with his illustrations. He manages to match the poetry, the silliness, the wisdom of the stories in his beautiful atmospheric pictures.
>
> —Axel Scheffler, author/illustrator

TULLET, HERVÉ

Translated from the French by Christopher Franceschelli

Press Here

Chronicle, 2011   ISBN: 9780811879545

Of Hervé Tullet's many brilliant (and award-winning) books, there's none better than *Press Here*. Both highly original and utterly simple, it creates a whole new degree of interaction between the reader and the printed object. Children (and, let's face it, adults) are encouraged to engage with the pictures by pressing, shaking, tilting the pages, and with each interaction the simple image is transformed – one dot becomes two, they change colour, grow and move. A delight to discover for the first time, yet whose low-tech tricks never seems to lose their appeal on re-reading. **2+**

VELTHUIJS, MAX

Translated from the Dutch by Anthea Bell

Frog in Love

Andersen Press, 2015 ISBN: 9781783441457

This picture book series – the best known work from the Dutch, Hans Christian Andersen Award winner, Max Velthuijs – features the philosophical and somewhat troubled anthropomorphic Frog. The books introduce profound existential thought, laying out sometimes complex themes for very young readers in a safe and sensitive way. *Frog and the Birdsong* is a beautifully simple account of death; *Frog Is Sad* is a touching depiction of depression; in *Frog in Love* our little green hero falls in love with Duck, and all ends well. **3+**

VINCENT, GABRIELLE

Translated from the French by Sam Alexander

Ernest and Celestine

Catnip, 2015 ISBN: 9781846471773

Monique Martin, alias Gabrielle Vincent, was a Belgian painter before becoming a writer and illustrator of books for children and adults. Her *nom de plume* is derived from the first names of her grandparents, Gabrielle and Vincent. This is the first of a series of beautiful books featuring, in sublime watercolour and ink images and minimal text, the daily life and friendship of Ernest the bear and Celestine the mouse. She takes her beloved toy penguin Simeon everywhere she goes, even as here, out for a walk in the snow with Ernest. But on the way home Celestine realises that she has dropped Simeon in the snow. Ernest promises to go and look for him the very next day as Celestine is inconsolable. A French 2D animated film based on this much loved series tells the tale of how they met and became such good friends. The film won the César for Best Animated Picture in 2013. **3+**

Riveting Reads: A World of Books in Translation

Where it all began...

myths, legends, fairy tales and fables

The first thing to say, perhaps, is that, if you're a reader of English, *most* fairy tales are translated fairy tales. The origins of those stories that fill our bedtime treasuries and inspire our fantasy writers and populate our picture books are almost all in other languages. (It's also worth mentioning that they're often not intended for children at all, but this isn't the place to go into that...)

From Frenchman Charles Perrault we got 'Cinderella', 'Little Red Riding Hood', 'Puss in Boots' and 'Sleeping Beauty'. From the German Brothers Grimm, 'Rapunzel', 'Hansel and Gretel', 'Rumpelstiltskin' and 'Snow White and the Seven Dwarfs'. Hans Christian Andersen in nineteenth-century Denmark gave us 'The Tinderbox', 'The Princess on the Pea', 'The Ugly Duckling' and 'The Little Mermaid'. Each of these stories found their way across to English – usually quite soon after they were recorded in French/German/Danish – and over the centuries they have been told and retold in this new language. They have continued to adapt over time, as fairy tales always do; and they have influenced the storytellers who came after them. Andersen's Snow Queen survives today not only in its countless English translations and versions of that story itself, but also in C.S. Lewis's White Witch, and in David Almond's *Kit's Wilderness*, and, for that matter, Disney's *Frozen*.

There are of course more collections of fairy tales than we could hope to do justice to in this guide. But even if we could include them all, that wouldn't begin to convey the ways the storytellers of the English-speaking world, have appropriated and transformed them. Roald Dahl included 'Little Red Riding Hood' in his *Revolting Rhymes*, though in his version the girl in question not only shoots and kills the wolf but ends up skinning the Three Little Pigs, too. In recent years the old 'Little Red Riding Hood' has given us many and various picture books and these are all, in their way, 'translations' of Perrault's story – just as Sondheim's *Into the Woods* is, too. They also all assume that we know some version of the original, against which each new version is playing; they assume, in other words, that these stories have become fully embedded in our own, Anglophone culture. The fact that their origins were once elsewhere is irrelevant now.

This is true for the Greek and Roman and Norse myths too; and for the Arabian Nights; and, for that matter, arguably for stories from the Bible to some extent. The 'translatedness' of their origins have been all but left behind – and so the stories themselves have a life that has far outgrown any notion of a once 'original' text. For many people today, the 'original' Snow White is the Disney one, not a fairy tale in German. As those specific European forebears recede further into the past, the connections between them and contemporary English writing stretch ever more thinly, and these new books are less like translations of originals texts and more like versions or retellings of infinitely flexible elemental stories that have transcended any original texts. Yes, Philip Pullman's *Fairy Tales from the Brothers Grimm* could be considered a 'translation' (though Pullman didn't work from the German); but what would you call Neil Gaiman's *The Sleeper and the Spindle*?

(It's probably also worth mentioning, at the risk of complicating things further, that even the stories we've referred to above – the Perraults, Grimms and Andersens – often don't actually have as clear-cut origins in one writer, place or language as we might suggest. Writers might not invent stories, they might merely capture stories that already exist, stories that have already travelled and evolved across many miles and centuries. The stories we ascribe to the Grimms are very often stories they collected rather than originated. Perrault's *Cinderella* is, yes, the early version we know best in English, but there are countless variants, starting in ninth-century China.)

So we have chosen to list some more or less faithful translations of foreign-language fairy tales; but also acknowledge their much wider influences with a list of other books, often more playful, that aren't translations in the strictest sense but which couldn't exist without a foreign book on which they are somehow based. Needless to say, even these are only the tiniest proportion of what we might have chosen.

Traditional Editions/Translations

Tales of Hans Christian Andersen
Translated by Naomi Lewis. Illustrated by Joel Stewart
Walker Books. ISBN: 9781406317466

The Complete Fairy Tales (Charles Perrault)
Translated by Christopher Betts
Oxford. ISBN: 9780199585809

The Complete Fairy Tales (The Brothers Grimm)
Translated by Jack Zipes
Vintage. ISBN: 9780099511441

Fairy Tales from the Brothers Grimm
Retold by Philip Pullman
Viking. ISBN: 9780670024971

Aesop: The Complete Fables
Translated by Robert and Olivia Temple
Penguin. ISBN: 9780140446494

Aesop's Fables
Retold by Fiona Waters. Illustrated by Fulvio Testa
Andersen Press. ISBN: 9781849392471

One Thousand and One Nights
Retold by C.J. Moore. Illustrated by Olga Dugina
Floris Books. ISBN: 9780863156007

The Penguin Book of Norse Myths: Gods of the Vikings
Retold by Kevin Crossley-Holland
ISBN: 9780241953211

Greek Myths
Retold by Ann Turnbull. Illustrated by Sarah Young
Walker. ISBN: 9781406339383

The Adventures of Hermes, God of Thieves: 100 Journeys through Greek Mythology
Muriel Szac. Translated by Mika Provota-Carlone
Pushkin Children's Books. ISBN: 9781782690306

The Orchard Book of Roman Myths
Retold by Geraldine McCaughrean. Illustrated by Emma Chichester Clark
ISBN: 9781843623083

Alternative Versions

Revolting Rhymes
Roald Dahl. Illustrated by Quentin Blake
Puffin. ISBN: 9780141369327

Tinder
Sally Gardner. Illustrated by David Roberts
Orion. ISBN: 9781780621487

A Thousand Nights
E.K. Johnston
Macmillan. ISBN: 9781447290377

The Sleeper and the Spindle
Neil Gaiman. Illustrated by Chris Riddell
Bloomsbury. ISBN: 9781408859643

I was a Rat: Or the Scarlet Slippers
Philip Pullman
Yearling. ISBN: 9780440866398

Little Red Hood
Marjolaine Leray. Translated by Sarah Ardizzone
Phoenix Yard Books. ISBN: 9781907912009

Little Red
Lynn Roberts. Illustrated by David Roberts
Pavilion. ISBN: 9781843651833

Little Red
Bethan Woollvin
Two Hoots. ISBN: 9781447291398

Little Red and the Very Hungry Lion.
Alex T. Smith
Scholastic. ISBN: 9781407143903

The Frog Prince (continued)
Jon Scieszka. Illustrated by Steve Johnson
Puffin. ISBN: 9780140542851

Prince Cinders
Babette Cole
Puffin. ISBN: 9780140555257

The Stinky Cheese Man and other Fairly Stupid Tales
Jon Scieszka. Illustrated by Lane Smith
Puffin. ISBN: 9780140548969

Goldilocks and Just the One Bear
Leigh Hodgkinson
Nosy Crow. ISBN: 9780857630445

8 to 12

AAKESON, KIM FUPZ

Translated from the Danish by Ruth Garde. Illustrated by Niels Bo Bojesen

Vitello Gets a Yucky Girlfriend

Pushkin Children's Books, 2013   ISBN: 9781782690030

Danish author Kim Fupz Aakeson has created a series of stories with a wonderful off-beat humour depicting the trials and tribulations of the mischievous but lovable rogue, Vitello. He lives in a terraced house on a noisy ring road with his long-suffering mother. Vitello doesn't play with girls (of course!) yet he is soon playing at being a robber who steals the princess' jewellery with Camilla, his new neighbour and her hamster. When things start to get too 'girly' Vitello is off, until, that is, he is persuaded to stay by the offer of biscuits. He doesn't have such a bad day after all playing with a girl but what does he do when Camilla suggests they become girlfriend and boyfriend? The plentiful cartoon-like illustrations really add to the appeal of these quirky tales. A best-seller series in Denmark, there are four other books about Vitello: *Vitello Scratches a Car, Vitello Becomes a Businessman, Vitello wants a Dad* and *Vitello carries a Knife*. **8+**

ATXAGA, BERNARDO

Translated from the Spanish by Margaret Jull Costa

Shola and the Lions

Pushkin Children's Books, 2015   ISBN: 9781782690641

The 2014 Marsh Award went to *The Adventures of Shola*, a quirky collection of four tales by Basque writer Bernardo Atxaga, translated by the always brilliant Margaret Jull Costa. These charming, witty, spirited stories describe the exploits of an irresistibly self-regarding little dog (she's really quite a character). In the hilarious *Shola and the Lions*, now published as a stand-alone volume, she is determined to prove that she is in fact a lion and not a dog – but it's not as easy as she expected. Shola is one of many treasures brought to us by Pushkin Children's Books, who of all the children's publishers in the UK today commission with the widest horizons. **8+**

AUBRY, CÉCILE

Translated from the French by Gregory Norminton. Illustrated by Helen Stephens

Belle and Sébastien: The Child of the Mountains

Alma Classics, 2016   ISBN: 9781847495914

Published in 1965 to coincide with the television series (also written by the French actress turned author), this is the timelessly appealing story of a young orphan boy who develops a strong bond with a stray Pyrenean mountain dog who is living wild in the mountains by his home, and sets out to save the dog before locals kill it. When Sébastien rescues the runaway Belle from the wrath of the villagers, the boy and the dog form a lifelong friendship and embark on exciting adventures in the mountains. The TV series became an international success and inspired the name of the now more famous pop group. This new edition is considerably enhanced by the beautiful illustrations. **8+**

BAISCH, MILENA

Translated from the German by Chantal Wright. Illustrated by Ellen Kusche

Anton and Piranha

Andersen Press, 2013 ISBN: 9781849396196

There's nothing better for livening up a potentially boring holiday with your grandparents than an encounter with a 'piranha'. In this case, the fish in question – caught by Anton's grandfather while fishing in the dark lake – becomes the boy's pet (well, more like his friend, really) and helps him get through the otherwise gruesome experience (camping, board games, and other similar horrors…). As much as anything, though, the book is about Anton's relationship with his grandparents, and the ways in which his holiday changes him – it's a charming story and very, very funny. **7+**

BERNA, PAUL

Translated from the French by John Buchanan-Brown. Illustrated by Richard Kennedy

A Hundred Million Francs

Puffin, 2016 ISBN: 9780141368719

This story of a bunch of scruffy urchins in the backstreets of Paris, who outwit thieves to uncover the whereabouts of millions of francs stolen from the Paris–Ventimiglia Express, has now achieved a permanent place among the outstanding books for children. In 1963 it was filmed by Walt Disney under the title *The Horse without a Head*. **9+**

> I found the hardback edition of Paul Berna's great adventure story set in Paris in the public library which we visited weekly. Like René Guillot's wonderful animal stories such as *The King of the Cats*, it was shelved alongside all the other books and no one mentioned that they had originally been written in another language. And I am sure I never thought of it; nor would I have cared if they had. So many stories were set 'in far off lands…' or 'long, long ago'; that was part of the point. In whatever place, the attraction was the story – children acting alone in a great city-set adventure in *A Hundred Million Francs* – and the pictures that accompanied it. In this case these were the fluent, loose-lined illustrations by Richard Kennedy who evoked the fading grandeur of streets of Paris. It was these, which included windows with shutters and seemingly endless flights of steps joining streets on different levels, that told me that the book was not set in my own London. The fact that the children had a mid-morning snack of bread with chocolate, then an unheard of but clearly delicious combination, added a pleasingly exotic touch.
>
> —Julia Eccleshare, children's books editor, *The Guardian*

BRAUN, DIETER

Translated from the German by Jen Calleja

Wild Animals of the North

Flying Eye, 2016 ISBN: 9781909263963

This is a beautiful illustrated guide, by an outstanding German artist, to some of the most magnificent and endangered animals that inhabit the northern hemisphere. The captivating, large scale illustrations are a mixture of digital media, pencil and watercolour where clean, simple geometric shapes build an incredibly accurate sense of the animals in their natural habitats, while the witty and idiosyncratic text adds a lively description of each backed up by some entertaining fun facts. There is also an illustrated index with cameo images of each animal at the back of the book. A visual feast that will stimulate interest in finding out more. **8+**

BRITT, FANNY

Translated from the French by Christelle Morelli and Susan Ouriou. Illustrated by Isabelle Arsenault

Jane, the Fox and Me

Walker, 2014   ISBN: 9781406353044

This first graphic novel collaboration between a Quebec playwright and an award-winning illustrator is a haunting, nuanced study of bullying, empathy, bravery and perseverance. The world for Hélène is currently drab and grey, shown by pencil scribbles, charcoal smudges and cloudy ink washes. Imagining her beloved Jane Eyre brings rare spots of colour, until the encounter with the fox when Hélène finds the confidence to trust a new friend, Géraldine, and real life takes on the full colour of fiction. An ultimately optimistic tale that sensitively explores the pain of isolation and shows how powerfully this format can tell a story. **9+**

COLLODI, CARLO

Translated from the Italian by Geoffrey Brock. Illustrated by Fulvio Testa

Pinocchio

Andersen Press, 2012   ISBN: 9781849392624

Carlo Collodi was the pen name of Carlo Lorenzini, who began his writing career as a journalist before turning to children's stories. He died in 1890, unaware of the international success that his creation Pinocchio would eventually enjoy. It was first translated into English in 1892 and there have been numerous translations and adaptations into English ever since. As well as having been translated into many other languages throughout the world, *Pinocchio* became internationally recognised when Walt Disney made a film of it in 1940. In this modern edition, Fulvio Testa's fifty full pages of sumptuous cartoon-like artwork help to lighten the tone, softening some of the darker scenes while enhancing the humour of the story of the mischievous puppet who longs to be a real boy.

You might also want to try the author's lesser known story **The Adventures of Pipì the Pink Monkey** (translated by Alessandro Gallenzi. Illustrated by Axel Scheffler. Alma Classics. ISBN: 9781847495594). **8+**

DE FOMBELLE, TIMOTHÉE

Translated from the French by Sarah Ardizzone. Illustrated by François Place

Toby Alone

Walker, 2009   ISBN: 9781406307269

This French teacher and successful playwright's first foray into writing children's books won the prestigious Marsh Award for translation and is an adventurous ecological fable with a hero who is a mere 1.5 millimetres tall, and whose entire world is contained within the branches of the great oak Tree. When his scientist father declares that the Tree is not only alive but also endangered by their civilization, the whole family is exiled, then arrested, then sentenced to death. Now Toby is running for his life and determined to save his parents. A fold-out map in the cover and many clever delicate illustrations add an extra element to this highly original fast-paced epic. Although Toby is small, his story is most definitely not, and readers will want to follow these characters into the sequel *Toby and the Secrets of the Tree* (2010. ISBN: 9781406325454). **9+**

DE SAINT-EXUPÉRY, ANTOINE
Translated from the French by Katherine Woods
The Little Prince
Egmont, 2001   ISBN: 9780749707231

An aviator, stranded in the Sahara Desert, encounters the Little Prince, a child who has fallen to earth from the asteroid where he is ruler and sole inhabitant. While the pilot is struggling to fix his plane, the boy shares his story: his asteroid world, a rose he once loved, his discoveries on earth. This magical book, an allegorical-symbolic exploration of the human condition, has over the years become one of the most widely loved children's books of all. **8+**

[Do also consider the rather lovely graphic novel version of this timeless tale: **The Little Prince**. (Adapted by Joann Sfar. Translated by Sarah Ardizzone. Walker. ISBN: 9781406331981.) Older readers who remember this classic with pleasure will be intrigued and not disappointed by **The Return of the Young Prince** imagined by the Argentinian author A.G. Roemmers. (Translated by Oliver Brock. Illustrated by Pietari Posti. Oneworld. ISBN: 9781780749563.)]

DIAS, MARIA ANA PEIXE AND DO ROSÁRIO, INÊS TEIXEIRA
Translated from the Portuguese by Lucy Greaves. Illustrated by Bernardo Carvalho
Outside: A Guide to Discovering Nature
Frances Lincoln, 2016   ISBN: 9781847807694

Unusual as it is for publishers to translate children's fiction, it's even less common for them to translate information books – *Outside* is a welcome rare exception. It's a celebration of the natural world that encourages children to explore and learn – it's densely packed with detailed information about butterflies and birds' nests and scallop shells and rainbows and all manner of other things. There are questions to think about and helpful tips and activities to do yourself; all in a big, attractively illustrated package. Enough to keep certain kids (and adults) engrossed for hours and hours. **8+**

DRAGT, TONKE
Translated from the Dutch by Laura Watkinson
The Letter for the King
Pushkin Children's Books, 2014   ISBN: 9781782690818

When sixteen-year-old Tiuri answers a desperate call for help, he finds himself on a perilous mission that could cost him his life. He must deliver a secret letter to the King who lives across the Great Mountains; a letter upon which the future of the entire realm depends. It means abandoning his home, breaking all the rules and leaving everything behind, even the knighthood that he has dreamed of for so long. First published in 1962 in the Netherlands, this wonderfully engrossing fantasy adventure received international recognition, translated into sixteen languages with over a million copies sold worldwide, and was also made into a feature film in 2008, but it took 52 years to reach the UK! It became the bestselling title from Pushkin Children's Books after an innovative marketing strategy leaving more than 100 copies on London Underground trains for people to discover. The books carried a letter for the reader, sealed with wax, with instructions to spread the word via mouth and social media, which they certainly did!

The enthralling sequel is *The Secret of the Wild Wood*. Newly published in November 2016 is a standalone title *The Song of Seven*. **10+**

Riveting Reads: A World of Books in Translation   8 to 12

> As a publisher who is also the father of three young children, there were few moments more thrilling than when I was reading an advance proof of Tonke Dragt's *The Letter for the King* to my son and older daughter and found that they literally couldn't wait for the next evening's chapter. So much so that early one morning my son actually sneaked into my bedroom when we were near the end and read the rest of it himself! What a joy to discover that this 1962 Dutch classic not only still resonated with English-speaking readers a half century later but had them completely and utterly gripped from first page to last. It's a testament to Tonke Dragt's skill as a storyteller and to the power of Laura Watkinson's brilliant translation.
>
> —Adam Freudenheim, Publisher, Pushkin Press

ENDE, MICHAEL

Translated from the German by Ralph Manheim

The Neverending Story

Puffin, 1984   ISBN: 9780140074314

One of the most popular German children's books of the twentieth century and adapted for film, opera, ballet and TV, this is the story of small, insignificant and unlikely hero Bastian Balthazar Bux. Through the pages of an old book he discovers Fantastika, a mysterious world of enchantment – but a world that is falling into decay. The great task of making things well again falls on Bastian. While his thrilling adventures will keep the pages turning, *The Neverending Story* isn't simply an imaginative fantasy but a story about the nature of imagination itself and what it really means for us human beings to dream or hope and even to wish. It is these underlying thought-provoking ideas that make this an enduring classic. **10+**

ENZENSBERGER, HANS MAGNUS

Translated from the German by Michael Henry Heim. Illustrated by Rotraut Susanne Berner

The Number Devil

Granta, 2008   ISBN: 9781847080530

An international best-seller, this is a very interesting and innovative book that has been described as 'making Pythagoras the new Harry Potter'. The book follows a young boy named Robert, who hates his maths teacher and the dull boring subject itself. But his dreams start to take on a life of their own as he is taught the principles of mathematics by a sly 'number devil' called Teplotaxl over the course of twelve exciting dreams. 'Hopefully, Mr Enzensberger's enterprising and imaginative book will play its part in rescuing some of Britain's children from a lifetime phobia of maths.'—*Daily Mail.* **8+**

FILIPOVIĆ, ZLATA

Translated from the Bosnian by Christina Pribichevich-Zoric

Zlata's Diary

Puffin, 1995   ISBN: 9780140374636

Zlata Filipović was given a diary, which she nicknamed Mimmy, shortly before her tenth birthday in 1991 and began to write in it regularly. Gradually it evolved from a fun and frivolous slice of pre-teen life complete with references to skiing trips, birthday parties, secret talks at sleepovers, pop music and fashion to a living testimony to some of the darkest times in recent history, the Bosnian War. Often inevitably compared to Anne Frank, Zlata's diary is a poignant record of a childhood lost to war and does indeed contain many descriptions of the horrors of war and both diaries take place during conflicts characterised by racism and ethnic cleansing. Fortunately for Zlata her diary was published initially by UNICEF during the conflict and became the means of escape from Sarajevo for her family. This modern classic remains a truly inspirational yet profoundly sad work that, much like the author at the time, has wisdom well beyond its years. **10+**

FUNKE, CORNELIA

Translated from the German by Anthea Bell

Inkheart

Chicken House, 2011   ISBN: 9781908435118

The first book in the award-winning German author's most famous trilogy is a book about booklovers written for booklovers. Who has not longed for characters to leap from the page or, better still, to be able to dive into an imagined world? Twelve-year-old Meggie learns that her father, Mo, who repairs and binds books for a living, can 'read' fictional characters to life. When she was three, he read aloud from a book called *Inkheart* and released characters into the real world. At the same time, Meggie's mother disappeared into the story. Now one of those characters abducts them and tries to force Mo into service to ensure he can stay in the real world. Thrilling drama, colourful characters and sheer unrelenting invention will keep readers committed throughout *Inkspell* and *Inkdeath*. **10+**

FURNARI, EVA

Translated from the Portuguese by Alison Entrekin. Illustrated by Moa Schulman

Fuzz McFlops

Pushkin Children's Books, 2015   ISBN: 9781782690757

Eva Furnari is one of Brazil's leading children's writers and has sold over 200,000 copies in Brazil of award-winning *Fuzz McFlops*, which tells the amusing tale of a reclusive poetry-writing rabbit who has been a loner ever since his classmates teased him for his lopsided ears in his youth. But a persistent female fan starts a correspondence and neither Fuzz's shyness nor his attacks of anxiety-induced ear spasmitis can prevent a beautiful friendship from forming. This is a wonderfully quirky warm-hearted tale, with endearing characters and delightfully amusing illustrations. The story is told with a highly entertaining mix of text, letters, postcards, instruction manual, poems, a song, patient information, a recipe, a fairy tale, a telegram and enhanced with beautiful and fitting illustrations. A joy to read for pleasure and just perfect for readers who love writing. **7+**

GOSCINNY, RENÉ

Translated from the French by Anthea Bell and Derek Hockridge. Illustrated by Albert Uderzo

Asterix the Gaul

Orion, 2005   ISBN: 9780752866055

Asterix is a diminutive, mustachioed Gaul who lives in a village in Brittany, 50BC. Together with such friends as Obelix, and with the aid of a magic potion made by the druid Getafix, Asterix manages to keep the Romans at bay. Much of the fun of the Asterix adventures lies in the names and other wordplay, which have been skillfully adapted in virtuosic English translations by Anthea Bell and Derek Hockridge. Other characters include Unhygienix the fishmonger, Cacofonix the Bard, and Dogmatix the dog (obviously). The stories first appeared in the French comic weekly *Pilote* in 1959, since when the Gauls' adventures have been published in many books. Following Goscinny's death in 1977, Uderzo continued to produce the albums alone, somewhat less successfully. The job has now passed down to a new team, with *Asterix and the Picts* by Jean-Yves Ferri and Didier Conrad album number 35 in the series, but thankfully the new titles continue to be translated by Anthea Bell. **8+**

GOSCINNY, RENÉ

Translated from the French by Anthea Bell. Illustrated by Jean-Jacques Sempé

Nicholas

Phaidon, 2011   ISBN: 9780714861142

These collections of humorous stories about a small boy and his experiences at school first appeared in French but have subsequently been widely translated and re-translated over the years. Each title is narrated by Nicholas himself, who tells his stories with perfect seriousness, so the reader is left to divine their humour. Nicholas always describes his friends in the same way, and they invariably behave in character: Alceste 'is fat and eats all the time'; Clotaire 'is bottom of the class'. In short chapters, each focusing on a particular adventure, the boys wreak chaos on the world without ever having any malicious intent. (And the clever child wins over the slow-witted adults every time.) Nicholas's antics are brought to life by the incisively comic illustrations of cartoonist Sempé. **8+**

GREDER, ARMIN

Translated from the German by Armin Greder

The Island

Allen & Unwin, 2005   ISBN: 9781741752663

Armin Greder's haunting *The Island* – considered by John Marsden 'one of my ten favourite picture books of all time' – is one of those books that (sadly) seems always to be relevant. A man gets himself washed up on an island, where the inhabitants are reluctant to make him welcome. Don't expect a happy ending. Muted illustrations and an economical text do nothing to diminish this book's power, its painfully eloquent message on identity, migration, xenophobia. It was followed by *The City*. **10+**

GRIMSTAD, LARS JOACHIM

Translated from the Norwegian by Don Bartlett and Siân Mackie

The Disappearing Children (Prime Minister Father and Son)

Phoenix Yard, 2015   ISBN: 9781907912382

The story begins when Finn's father, a taxi driver, rather surprisingly becomes Prime Minister of Norway. (Having spent years listening to his passengers grumbling away in the back, he knows *exactly* what the electorate wants.) Which may seem a promising beginning for Finn, but it all starts going wrong when the children in his class start disappearing… This book, the first in a series, was the debut of a one-time professional footballer, and it's got everything a reader could wish for: an exciting story, great characters, humour, weirdness, robots, and even a bit of political satire mixed in. **9+**

GRIPARI, PIERRE
Translated from the French by Sophie Lewis. Illustrated by Puig Rosado
The Good Little Devil and Other Tales
Pushkin Children's Books, 2013   ISBN: 9781782690085

It's taken nearly fifty years for these internationally bestselling stories to find their way into English. The thirteen magical tales are original and offbeat, and quite consistently odd – a potato and a Sultan fall in love, a pig swallows the Pole Star, a great hero gets no credit for his heroic deeds because his name's just too awful – in ways that children readily accept without any of our silly grown-up prejudice against such things, and they're written and translated with humour and charm. **9+**

HERGÉ
Translated from the French by Leslie Lonsdale-Cooper and Michael Turner
The Adventures of Tintin
Egmont, 2015   ISBN: 9781405282758

In these much-loved, and regularly adapted, books from Belgian master cartoonist Hergé (Georges Remi), Tintin is a teenage reporter-cum-amateur-detective who gets embroiled in every kind of thriller-adventure, along with his dog Snowy ('Milou' in the original French), the coincidently named plain-clothes and dimwitted policemen Thomson and Thompson (originally Dupont and Dupond), the stormy Captain Haddock ('Thundering typhoons! Billions of blue blistering barnacles!'), and the deaf and absent-minded Professor Cuthbert Calculus. Tintin has, at various times, visited the moon, gone in search of pirate treasure, crossed the desert, and in *King Ottakar's Sceptre* (originally published in 1939), become involved in political shenanigans which bear a resemblance to European events during the 1930s. The unusual freshness of plot and dialogue, combined with some absurd characters and humour, have made these old books endure incredibly well. **8+**

HOLM, ANNE
Translated from the Danish by L.W. Kingsland
I Am David
Egmont, 2000   ISBN: 9780749701369

First published in Danish as *David*, this is the powerful story of a twelve-year-old boy escaping from the unnamed eastern European concentration camp where he has lived his whole life, and journeying across Europe to Denmark, learning about the outside world along the way. It's dark at times, but at its heart it's about David's own discovery of beauty, kindness and strength, in himself and others. An exciting story, but also rich in emotion and compassion, this one has gripped readers for over half a century. **10+**

HUB, ULRICH
Translated from the German by Helena Ragg-Kirby. Illustrated by Jorgen Muhle
Meet at the Ark at Eight
Pushkin Children's Books, 2015   ISBN: 9781782690870

Of all the books about a penguin in a suitcase pretending to be God asking for a cheesecake, *Meet at the Ark at Eight* is absolutely, definitely my favourite. It's the quirky tale of three penguins on Noah's ark debating the existence of God and trying to keep out of trouble. And it's as funny – and unique – as it sounds. A slim book filled with philosophical ideas and theological enquiry, it's a lovely one to read to younger children. Yes, really. **7+**

HWANG, SUN-MI

Translated from the Korean by Chi-Young Kim. Illustrated by Kazuko Nomoto

The Hen Who Dreamed She Could Fly

Oneworld, 2014   ISBN: 9781780745343

Often described as Korea's answer to *Charlotte's Web*, this international bestseller is the story of Sprout, a hen who decides she wants more out of life. She wants to get away from the farmyard, to a place where she might hatch an egg of her own, rather than having them all taken away from her to market. It's not as simple as it seems, however, not least because most of the other animals in the farmyard – the duck excepted – are far from friendly. *The Hen Who Dreamed She Could Fly* is a poignant little fable about freedom, courage, maternal love and following your dreams. **10+**

INUI, TOMIKO

Translated from the Japanese by Ginny Tapley Takemori

The Secret of the Blue Glass

Pushkin Children's Books, 2015   ISBN: 9781782690344

This is the first of this award-winning Japanese author's books to be translated into English and it tells the story of the Moriyama family who have been entrusted by a returning English governess with the safekeeping of a family of Little People down the generations. When war comes to Tokyo, will little Yuri still be able to fulfil the promise of her family and ensure the blue goblet is filled with milk each evening? The fantasy is obviously reminiscent of *The Borrowers,* and there is also the cheeky little imp Amanejakki and a couple of talking pigeons. However all this is set against the backdrop of the very real events of the Second World War from a Japanese perspective with historical detail of the hardship experienced by ordinary Japanese families and the dangers presented by the British origins of the Little People – a very subtle warning about the dangers of fanatical nationalism. Altogether an unusual, charming and deeply moving book, which became the first translated book ever to be nominated for the Carnegie Medal after the change to the eligibility criteria in 2015. **8+**

JANSSON, TOVE

Translated from the Swedish by Elizabeth Portch

Finn Family Moomintroll

Puffin, 2009   ISBN: 9780141353449

This was the third book this Hans Christian Andersen Award-winning author wrote about these characters, but the first to be translated into English and this was the book which brought her worldwide fame, leading as it did to a Moomin comic strip for London's *Evening News* newspaper. It was an instant hit and within two years 120 newspapers around the world were running it, reaching 12 million readers. Jansson was Finnish but she wrote the books in Swedish and did all the illustrations herself. This classic series seems never to age and the amusing antics of the Moomin family and their friends remain as enjoyable today as when they were written. **7+**

> First translated in 1950, I was just the right age – a few years later – to borrow this from my local library. The delightful Moomins and their eccentric, fantastic, gentle adventures may have been my first experience of fantasy (a lifelong love!) Even as a child I was aware of the gentle fun being made between the characters, whilst always being aware of the welcoming and soothing presence of Moominmama looking after everyone.
>
> —Tricia Adams, director, School Library Association

JUNG, REINHARDT

Translated from the German by Anthea Bell

Bambert's Book of Missing Stories

Egmont, 2008   ISBN: 9781405236409

You might imagine Bambert's life was a sad and solitary one – living alone in his attic flat, finding it hard to move around, with food sent up by his bemused but kindly downstairs neighbour in a special lift… – but then you'd be underestimating the power of stories. Because Bambert's apparently simple life is rich in those! His intense imaginative dream-world provides the fuel for the stories he writes, and which he then sends floating off, attached to tiny hot-air balloons, to find their place in the world. An unusual story with an unusual hero, and a rather magical one. **8+**

KAABERBØL, LENE

Translated from the Danish by Charlotte Barslund. Illustrated by Rohan Eason

Wildwitch: Wildfire

Pushkin Children's Books, 2016   ISBN: 9781782690832

This is the first in the 'Wildwitch' series and won the ORLA prize, the biggest Danish children's book award. Clara is a normal twelve-year-old girl, until a scary encounter with an unusually large black cat changes her life forever. With the help of her Aunt Isa, she is introduced to her astounding true nature: as a Wildwitch, she can learn to communicate with animals, and harness the magical power of the natural world around her. Followed by *Oblivion, Life Stealer* and *Bloodling*, this series will appeal to all fantasy fans, and deserves to become a classic. **9+**

KÄSTNER, ERICH

Translated from the German by Eileen Hall. Illustrated by Walter Trier

Emil and the Detectives

Red Fox Classic, 2004   ISBN: 9780099413127

Erich Kästner, from Dresden in Germany, was born the son of a saddle-maker and a maid in 1899. His early experience conscripted to the army was to influence his pacifism all his life. *Emil and the Detectives* published in 1928 was a great success. A sequel, *Emil and the Three Twins*, appeared in 1933, but soon afterwards his books were labelled 'contrary to the German spirit' and burned in public by the Nazis. This classic tale of a boy turned detective in order to track down a thief has recently also been successfully adapted for the National Theatre. **8+**

> Some of my favourite books when I was a child were written in languages other than English: the Père Castor picture books, *Pinocchio*, a Russian story called 'A White Sail Gleams', folk tales from around the world – Russia, France, Germany – especially the rogue tales about 'Till Eulenspiegel'. My particular favourite was *Emil and the Detectives*, a wonderful evocation of what it means for a country boy to arrive in the big city. The big city in question is Berlin in the 1920s and Kästner makes it lit up, jazzy, free and above all full of help from street kids who help him catch the man who stole his money. The book is told in several ways at the same time, an ordinary impersonal narration alongside personal author-to-reader vignettes where it's as if Kästner takes us to one side and lets us in on who's who.
>
> —Michael Rosen, author and poet

KÄSTNER, ERICH

Translated from the German by Anthea Bell. Illustrated by Walter Trier

The Flying Classroom

Pushkin Children's Books, 2014   ISBN: 9781782690566

The German children's writer Erich Kästner is best known in this country for *Emil and the Detectives*, but he wrote many more books for children. Two of the best, *The Flying Classroom* and *The Parent Trap* (yes, the one adapted into that film) have lately been revived, with the original illustrations by Walter Trier, and fresh life breathed into them with bright new translations by Anthea Bell. In *The Flying Classroom*, we meet Martin and his schoolfriends, for what might *look* like a typical school story, but really isn't… **8+**

LAGERCRANTZ, ROSE

Translated from the Swedish by Julia Marshall. Illustrated by Eva Eriksson

My Happy Life

Gecko Press, 2012   ISBN: 9781877467806

The first of a delightful series of short chapter books from Sweden featuring the gentle Dani who likes to be happy even when life makes it hard to do so. She is always full of optimism and probably the happiest person she knows. Life gets even better when she starts school and meets Ella who becomes her best friend. They do everything together and life is great fun. Then one day Ella moves away and Dani becomes sad and lonely as she faces the challenge of how to remain happy. Dani's story continues in *My Heart Is Laughing*, *When I Am Happiest* and *Life According to Dani*. The warm and wonderful illustrations really bring these touching and amusing tales to life. **6+**

LAGERLÖF, SELMA

Translated from the Swedish by Paul Norlen

The Wonderful Adventure of Nils Holgersson

Penguin Classics, 2016   ISBN: 9780241206089

Selma Lagerlöf was the first woman to win the Nobel Prize for literature in 1909 and this has been described as Scandinavia's favourite children's classic. It has been translated into over 40 languages and made into films and animations. Written at the request of the Swedish National Teachers Society, this is the story of a mischievous fourteen-year-old who is changed into a tiny elf able to understand the language of animals; transported across the Swedish countryside on the back of a goose, he learns about nature, geography, and folklore. Each chapter is an individual story, often a retelling of a fairy tale or myth with Nils and his animals as the protagonists. There are also important lessons for Nils to learn such as compassion, justice and respect for nature. If all this sounds rather worthy rest assured that the author's genius is to make the storytelling and the characters truly enchanting. **8+**

LINDGREN, ASTRID

Translated from the Swedish by Tiina Nunnally. Illustrated by Lauren Child

Pippi Longstocking

Oxford University Press, 2012   ISBN: 9780192758231

This beautiful edition of the children's classic is illustrated throughout with wonderful collage pictures from the award-winning Lauren Child, which are the perfect match for this most famous Swedish export. Pippi Longstocking has encouraged countless girls to believe in themselves, both in Sweden and abroad. Nine-year-old Pippi lives all by herself in Villa Villekulla with a horse, a monkey called Mr Nilsson and a big suitcase full of gold coins. A unique and feisty child, she soon makes it clear to the grown-ups in the village that she has no intention of conforming. She has other ideas, much preferring to spend her days arranging exciting adventures or entertaining her next-door neighbours Tommy and Annika with her outrageous stories. Generations of children have fallen in love with Pippi Longstocking and will inevitably continue to do so. **7+**

LINDGREN, ASTRID

Translated from the Swedish by Patricia Crampton

Ronia, the Robber's Daughter

Oxford University Press, 2010   ISBN: 9780192789945

This is perhaps my own favourite Astrid Lindgren, and it also comes from the pen of the translator who brought us so many of her works (and so much else besides), the great Patricia Crampton. It's the story of two feuding robber clans, who live in two halves of the same castle (split in half by a lightning-bolt), and a girl called Ronia who by befriending a boy from the rival gang manages finally to bring them together. There's plenty of adventure, a strong and spirited main character, and some truly magical storytelling. **7+**

LINDGREN, ASTRID

Translated from the Swedish by Joan Tate. Illustrated by Ilon Wikland

The Brothers Lionheart

Oxford University Press, 2009   ISBN: 9780192729040

When Jonathan and Karl Lion both die tragically, they find themselves transported to the world of Nangyala. When their idyll comes under threat, it is up to the boys to help protect it. Brave, bold Jonathan instantly steps up to the mark, but can shy, frail Karl prove himself in the ultimate fight against evil and show that he truly is a Lionheart? This fantasy story is rather different to the stories Lindgren is best known for today and certainly with less emphasis on comedy and the everyday, instead transporting us to a new world which is both similar and different to our own and the site of an epic struggle between good and evil. **9+**

> I have read and loved all of Astrid Lindgren's books. This one was always my favourite. Is there any other children's book that talks so fearlessly about death? And takes the fear of it with such ease. But there is so much more. What do we have to do when we meet cruelty and injustice? What makes a good man? And child? Is violence needed to fight violence? What does it feel like to be betrayed by a friend? I don't think anyone who ever met the brothers Lionheart will be able to forget them.
> —Cornelia Funke, author

MAGNASON, ANDRI SNÆR

Translated from the Icelandic by Julian Meldon D'Arcy. Illustrated by Áslaug Jónsdóttir

The Story of the Blue Planet

Pushkin Children's Books, 2015   ISBN: 9781782690658

This was the first children's book to win the Icelandic Literary Prize and then it became the first book on the new Pushkin children's list, before becoming the first translated book to win the UKLA Book Award for seven to eleven-year-olds. Brimir and Hulda are best friends, living on a beautiful blue planet where there are no grown-ups. Life is wild and free, and each day is more exciting than the last. Until, one day, a rocket ship piloted by a strange-looking adult named Gleesome Goodday crashes on the beach. He promises endless fun, but they don't realise that this gift comes at a price for themselves and the rest of their planet. This is a magical cautionary ecological tale which also makes you question whether it is ethical to be happy at the expense of others' suffering. **9+**

MAUROIS, ANDRÉ
Translated from the French by Norman Denny. Illustrated by Fritz Wegner
Fattypuffs and Thinifers
Vintage, 2013 ISBN: 9780099582922

Two boys travel underground to a pair of enemy kingdoms, inhabited by Fattypuffs and Thinifers, respectively: the very thin Thinifers obey a rule of life which means 'going without lunch and working six days a week'; the fat and lazy Fattypuffs are interested only in eating and sleeping. It's a terrifically fun story, funny and full of pleasingly surreal inventiveness; but it's Fritz Wegner's hilarious, irresistible illustrations that make it for me. (Wegner, who died in 2015, was never the household name he deserved to be, even if his illustrations are recognisable to anyone who's seen them.) They do that thing all great illustrations do, making it quite impossible to imagine the story existing without them. **9+**

> Two underground countries; conflict and ultimate concord between populations, one obese and lazy, the other painfully thin and driven; a Franco-German parable: the deliciously prescient *Patapoufs et Filifers* (1930) is still pertinent, and it's very funny and very stylish. The perfect hors d'oeuvre to Maurois' wonderful essays on *The Art of Living* (1940).
> —Kevin Crossley-Holland, author, poet and president of the School Library Association

MERCIER, JOHANNE
Translated from the French by Daniel Hahn
Arthur and the Mystery of the Egg
Phoenix Yard, 2013 ISBN: 9781907912160

Meet seven-year-old Arthur, the delightful hero in the first of a series of witty tales with a twist and a set of strong family relationships at their heart. French Canadian author Johanne Mercier has created a very real seven year old who here is trying to solve the age old mystery of 'Which came first, the chicken or the egg?' Everything is seen through Arthur's eyes which will appeal directly to young readers. The language is easily accessible to children but contains a degree of irony that will be enjoyed by adults too and both will be keen to read more. **5+**

MIZIELIŃSKA, ALEKSANDRA AND MIZIELIŃSKI, DANIEL
Translated from the Polish by Antonia Lloyd-Jones
Under Earth, Under Water
Templar, 2016 ISBN: 9781783703647

A few years ago, a gorgeous and immensely stylish large-format illustrated book called *Maps*, from Polish illustrating double-act Aleksandra Mizielińska and Daniel Mizieliński, was a surprise hit in the UK publishing world. Well, now the couple are back – and once again teamed up with translator Antonia Lloyd-Jones – with another book, which is perhaps more impressive still. *Under Earth, Under Water* takes readers on a thrilling journey underground and beneath the seas (the book itself, a beautiful object, moves either down under the earth or down under the water depending on which side you open it from). Each page of the book is so beautifully put together, the artwork and the colour so rich, it's easy not to notice how informative it all is, too. Stunning. **7+**

MODIANO, PATRICK

Translated from the French by William Rodarmor. Illustrated by Jean-Jacques Sempé

Catherine Certitude

Andersen Press, 2014   ISBN: 9781783443024

Catherine, the eponymous heroine, begins her story watching her own daughter demonstrate jazz steps in their ballet school on a snowy afternoon in New York. Memory takes her (and the reader) back to her childhood, spent with her father in the tenth arrondissement of Paris in the 1950s. He runs a shipping business in Paris with a failed poet named Casterade. Father and daughter share the simple pleasures of daily life: sitting in the church square, walking to school, going to her ballet class every Thursday afternoon. But just why did Georges change his name to Certitude? What kind of trouble with the law did Casterade rescue him from? And why did Catherine's ballerina mother leave to return to New York? The only children's story by 2014's winner of the Nobel Prize in Literature and beautifully illustrated, this is an elegantly written love letter to Paris, ballet and childhood. **10+**

> As a publisher I am very disappointed in the number of translations available in Britain. I publish fewer now, as sales are always disappointing. Modiano, last year's Nobel Prize winner, wrote a very lovely children's book entitled *Catherine Certitude* which had a small number of great reviews but sold only 2,200 copies. Britain still seems insular. But recently there appears to be more interest in buying titles from abroad and I suspect next year will see an increase.
> —Klaus Flugge, publisher

MOERS, WALTER

Translated from the German by John Brownjohn

The 13½ Lives of Captain Bluebear

Vintage, 2001   ISBN: 9780099285328

Don't be put off by the vast size of this one – some readers may think it looks daunting, but as soon as you're into it, it's such fun! The title character is an old sea-going bear (yes, he's blue), who shares the fantastical adventures of his buccaneering 13½ lives (bluebears have 27 lives, as everybody knows, so this is supposed to cover the first half). His travels bring him into contact with some brilliantly inventive worlds and creatures, some pre-existing and others entirely original to this book. It's all rather hard to describe, but think *Hitchhiker* meets *Gulliver*. Moers himself is a distinguished cartoonist as well as writer and his pictures add extra humour and charm to the story. **9+**

NESBØ, JO

Translated from the Norwegian by Tara Chace. Illustrated by Mike Lowery

Doctor Proctor's Fart Powder

Simon & Schuster, 2015   ISBN: 9781471125447

Fans of Nesbø's adult crime novels will be surprised to learn that this sold more copies in his native Norway than any other children's debut. Now a major film and translated into more than 40 languages it tells the story of Doctor Proctor who has finally created something to help him fulfil his dream of becoming a famous inventor – a super-strength fart powder that can propel people into outer space! But ruthless twins Truls and Trym are determined to spoil the Doctor's plans, sparking a fart-filled adventure involving a firework extravaganza, a trip to prison and an escaped anaconda. There is so much more than the obvious scatological humour for children and adults to enjoy in this series with parody, satire, and some very witty dialogue. **8+**

NILSSON, ULF

Translated from the Swedish by Julia Marshall. Illustrated by Gitte Spee

Detective Gordon: The First Case

Gecko Press, 2015   ISBN: 9781927271506

Written by an award-winning Swedish writer who has published more than 100 books and picture books and is president of the Swedish Academy for Children's Books, this is a brilliant example of the classic odd couple/buddy detectives trope we know from films but in a beautifully simple text with exquisite watercolour illustrations. Detective Gordon (a toad) is the chief of police in the forest and young, irrepressible Buffy (a mouse) is his brand-new sidekick. Using their complementary skills, they track down some nut thieves and mete out the appropriate justice. Full of gentle humour, warmth and wisdom. **7+**

NÖSTLINGER, CHRISTINE

Translated from the German by Anthea Bell

The Factory Made Boy

Andersen Press, 2012   ISBN: 9781849394833

Christine Nöstlinger is one of the best children's writers of our time, but she's practically unknown in the UK. This is one I remember from my own childhood reading, a brilliantly funny story about conformity (or otherwise). In it, a rather eccentric woman, Mrs Bartolotti, receives a parcel in the post containing a factory-made child called Conrad, who is perfect in every way (and much better behaved, frankly, than his new parent); but the factory have made a mistake and soon they want him back… **9+**

OHLSSON, KRISTINA

Translated from the Swedish by Marlaine Delargy

The Glass Children

Jonathan Cape, 2014   ISBN: 9780857551429

Billie and her widowed mother have just moved into a new house, in the hope of a new start in life, but there's definitely something strange about the place. Something creepy going on – but what? It's as though someone, or something, were trying to scare them away. Billie and her new friend Aladdin soon get caught up in an ever-twisting, ghostly mystery, with dark long-buried secrets just waiting to be revealed… Tautly plotted and atmospheric, *The Glass Children* is a gripping and unsettling read. **10+**

PARR, MARIA

Translated from the Norwegian by Guy Puzey. Illustrated by Kate Forrester

Waffle Hearts

Walker, 2014   ISBN: 9781406347906

Waffle Hearts may be set in a small town in Scandinavia, but it almost feels as though it might be anywhere. Yes, the setting is vivid and culturally precise, but the irresistibly appealing story is about friendship and multi-generational family and community, told with great humour and warmth, reminding us what we have in common, not what keeps us apart. In it we meet Trille and Lina, neighbours (and best friends) at their homes in Mathildewick Cove, and with tears and laughter we watch their wild adventures unfold. Utterly lovely. **9+**

> For a publisher looking for good writing to translate, one obvious criterion is the recognition the book may have in its original language. When I was shown *Waffle Hearts* it hadn't just won acclaim in Norway but the Dutch had awarded the Zilveren Griffel and the French the Prix Sorcières and many other countries had already translated it. Looking for a translator can be tricky, but in this case Guy Puzey had already translated some pages and Maria loved his work. It was the beginning of a very good story in every way. *Waffle Hearts* is a joyful and timeless tale set in a seaside cove in Norway. Lena is a treasure of a smart, fearless girl living a very real life, with sadness as well as crazy adventures in her world. The warmth, fine observation and humour in this story, set in a landscape which recalls Lindgren and Jansson, give it a classic appeal and it deservedly now has many English-speaking fans around the world.
>
> —Gill Evans, publisher

PENNAC, DANIEL

Translated from the French by Sarah Adams (Sarah Ardizzone). Illustrated by Max Grafe

The Eye of the Wolf

Walker, 2014   ISBN: 9781406352573

This highly original story about suffering, courage and growing friendship was the first of this celebrated French author's works to be translated into English. The wolf has lost nearly everything on his journey to the zoo, including an eye and his beloved pack. The boy too has lost much and seen many terrible things. They stand eye to eye on either side of the wolf's enclosure and, slowly, each makes his own extraordinary story known to the other. The superb writing keeps an intense hold over readers, and the subtle shades of the black and white illustrations blur the lines of the real and surreal events. **9+**

PLICHOTA, ANNE AND WOLF, CENDRINE

Translated from the French by Sue Rose

Oksa Pollock: The Last Hope

Pushkin Children's Books, 2014   ISBN: 9781782690351

This is the first of a series of six fantasy children's novels written by a French author duo of ex-librarians that was a self-published sensation in France before selling millions worldwide. The series follows Oksa Pollock, a young girl who has just moved to London with her family. She lives the life of an average thirteen-year-old girl until her grandmother reveals that she was previously a resident and princess of the land of Edefia and now Oksa has inherited her powers and is the 'Last Hope' against the dangerous group known as the Felons threatening the kingdom. With colourful characters, a feisty heroine, strange creatures and eccentric details this is an enormously appealing fantasy world. **10+**

PREUSSLER, OTFRIED

Translated from the German by Anthea Bell

Krabat

The Friday Project, 2010   ISBN: 9780007395118

A quarter of a century before J.K. Rowling first imagined Harry Potter, the great Otfried Preussler gave us a boy called Krabat who is surprised to find himself enrolled in a magic school and brought face to face with some very dark forces… This one is set in the eighteenth century, where the master to whom he is apprenticed is bound by a terrible pact. (The 'school' is a darker and more threatening place than Hogwarts ever was.) Filled with excitement and peril, atmosphere and action, it's a captivating look at the temptations of power and evil… **10+**

PRØYSEN, ALF

Translated from the Norwegian by Marianne Helweg

Mrs Pepperpot to the Rescue and Other Stories

Red Fox, 2012   ISBN: 9781849418027

Old Mrs Pepperpot frequently finds she has shrunk to the size of a pepperpot – and it always seems to happen when she least expects it! In Alf Prøysen's classic stories she tackles all manner of troubles (including a huge ice-cream mountain!), she often befriends animals along the way (she can talk to them), and she's always safely returned to human size by the end. Prøysen wrote many dozens of stories about this much-loved character, brought together in a number of collections, and they are consistently magical. (In the Norwegian, incidentally, she is 'Teskjekjerringa', the 'teaspoon woman'. The 'pepperpot' name is the translator's.) **7+**

SALTEN, FELIX

Translated from the German by Whittaker Chambers. Illustrated by Richard Cowdrey

Bambi: A Life in the Woods

Simon & Schuster, 2013   ISBN: 9781442467453

This most famous work of the Austrian writer, born Siegmund Salzmann, was a huge international success on its publication in 1923, with the movie rights acquired by Walt Disney for the 1942 animated film, and yet few people know that it was banned in Nazi Germany in 1936 as 'political allegory on the treatment of Jews in Europe'. Certainly this unforgettable story with its harsh and terrifying account of the deaths caused by human hunters is nothing like Disney, but it is a beautifully written and moving paean to nature and Salten is able to perform that rare trick of expertly depicting real animals we can empathise with without adding human personalities. **10+**

SANDÉN, MÅRTEN
Translated from the Swedish by Karin Altenberg. Illustrated by Moa Schulman
A House without Mirrors
Pushkin Children's Books, 2013   ISBN: 9781782690078

Eleven-year-old Thomasine has spent months living in her great-great-aunt Henrietta's rambling old house with her dysfunctional family. The odd thing about this house is that there are no mirrors anywhere. In fact, the house holds an incredible secret. When Thomasine's five-year-old cousin Signe makes a discovery; a wardrobe full of mirrors through which you can step into a different world, everything changes as each member of the family, including Thomasine and her father learn something from their experience in the wardrobe of mirrors and their lives are changed forever. This hauntingly, beautiful tale of love, loss and family relationships is from one of Sweden's bestselling children's authors. **9+**

SCHMIDT, ANNIE M.G.
Translated from the Dutch by David Colmer
The Cat Who Came in off the Roof
Pushkin Children's Books, 2016   ISBN: 9781782690979

Written in 1970 by Dutch author Annie M.G. Schmidt, who won the Hans Christian Andersen Award in 1989, this quaint tale is a true classic. The characterisation of the cats is so well defined and the humour, particularly from Minou and her cat-like behaviour, is very endearing. **8+**

The Cat Who Came in off the Roof is about a cat named Minou who mysteriously turns into a woman, and a man called Tibble who works for the newspaper and is about to lose his job. Fortunately, when he takes in Minou, she collects news stories from local cats and Tibble's job is safe – for the meantime, that is. Soon there is a car crash, and they uncover a dark side of the Mayor, Mr Ellmore! But no one believes Tibble, and he must convince everyone that cats are witnesses, with some help from Minou! I like Minou because she is a very brave person and is kind to everyone. She may be a bit shy and odd to Tibble at first, but she soon becomes friends with many people – and cats!

—Emily Malone, book reviewer (aged 9)

SEPÚLVEDA, LUIS
Translated from the Spanish by Margaret Sayers Peden. Illustrated by Satoshi Kitamura
The Story of a Seagull and the Cat Who Taught Her to Fly
Alma Books, 2016   ISBN: 9781846884009

Born in Santiago, Chile, Luis Sepúlveda is the multi-award-winning author of many adult novels and stories for children. Politically and socially engaged, he was persecuted and jailed by the Pinochet regime and worked for years as a crew member on a Greenpeace ship. This heart-warming story of interspecies cooperation with a strong environmental message has been translated in over 40 countries with several film and theatre adaptations. The lovely illustrations perfectly catch both the humour and the pathos of this beautifully written fable. **8+**

SPYRI, JOHANNA

Translated from the German by Eileen Hall

Heidi

Puffin, 2009   ISBN: 9780141322568

This Swiss classic, first published in 1891, has been a worldwide bestseller with many film and TV adaptations. The story of the orphan sent to live with her reclusive grandfather on his mountain, her friendship with the goatherd Peter, being sent to stay in Frankfurt and then triumphant homecoming and the healing of poor Clara is as affecting and engaging a story as ever. The evocative depictions of the mountain life, landscape and people and Heidi's indomitable and endearing character ensure its classic status. It was one of the first books to celebrate the way children see the world around them and was intended, according to Spyri, as 'a story for children and those who love children.' **8+**

> I can't express the importance of books from all over the world in the words allowed. But I can pass on the wonder of reading *Heidi* – a book recently 'borrowed' from my shelf by a young neighbour and not coming back any time soon. Heidi was my friend and I wanted to live with Grandfather high up in the Swiss Alps. Her story of friendship, love, jealousy, social upheaval and more is as relevant now as it was when published in 1879. I loved it – and the new world it allowed me to enter.
> —Wendy Cooling, freelance book consultant and SLA patron

STAROBINETS, ANNA

Translated from the Russian by Jane Bugaeva. Illustrated by Andrezj Klimowski

Catlantis

Pushkin Children's Books, 2015   ISBN: 9781782690887

This is the first children's novel from this acclaimed Russian author to be translated into English. It is the wonderfully whimsical and witty tale of Baguette, a self-obsessed house cat whose task is to voyage back through the Ocean of Time to find the lost island of Catlantis and the magical Catlantis flower, which will save the nine lives of all cats, in order to win the paw of his lady love, the beautiful street cat Purriana. Full of clever cat puns and striking black and white illustrations, this is a feline myth worthy of comparison with Plato's original story of Atlantis. **9+**

STEINHÖFEL, ANDREAS

Translated from the German by Chantal Wright. Illustrated by Steven Wells

The Pasta Detectives

Chicken House, 2010   ISBN: 9781906427276

Andreas Steinhöfel's immensely likeable novel is a kind of mystery story, but far quirkier than that description might suggest. Although young Rico (our friendly narrator) and Oscar (who always wears a big crash helmet) are both outsiders in their Berlin world, they otherwise could not be more different; but they do become friends somehow, and when Oscar disappears all of a sudden it falls to the highly observant Rico to work out what has happened. Is his friend the latest victim of a kidnapping plot that's been going on in the neighbourhood? Both hilarious and touching, *The Pasta Detectives* is a story of fear and bravery, and of friendship. (It's hardly about pasta at all.) **8+**

WALSH, MARÍA ELENA

Translated from the Spanish by Daniel Hahn. Illustrated by Aurora Cacciapuoti

An Elephantasy

Pushkin Children's Books, 2016   ISBN: 9781782690993

María Elena Walsh was an Argentinian poet, novelist, musician, playwright, writer and composer, mainly known for her songs and books for children. She was highly commended for the Hans Christian Andersen Prize, and one of the songs she wrote became a civil rights anthem during the military dictatorship in Argentina. Full of gentle surreal nonsense in the great tradition of Edward Lear, this story is set in a reality where fantastical things like an elephant called Dalian Kafki turning up at the door of the female narrator and her family can just happen. Naturally she feels she has no choice but to adopt him despite the obvious complications, and that is just the beginning of her adventures. Featured in *1001 Children's Books You Must Read before You Grow up*, this international bestseller is a true delight. **9+**

12 to 14

ACIOLI, SOCORRO

Translated from the Portuguese by Daniel Hahn

The Head of the Saint

Hot Key Books, 2014   ISBN: 9781471402906

This young Brazilian author was selected to take part in a writing workshop with Gabriel García Márquez on the basis of the synopsis of this fascinating novel, full of Brazilian atmosphere and culture and more than a little magical realism. Samuel's dying mother asks him to light candles at the feet of three saints. This request sends Samuel on a journey on foot, which will lead him to an ill-fated village. He finds shelter in the fallen head of a statue of a saint. And soon, he discovers that he can hear the villagers' whispered prayers to Saint Anthony and he begins to wonder if he ought to help them out a little. When Samuel's advice hits the mark he becomes famous, and people flock to the town to hear about their future loves. But with all the fame comes some problems, and soon Samuel has more than just the lovelorn to deal with. A captivating novel, told in spare, elegant prose. **13+**

BARROUX

Translated from the French by Sarah Ardizzone

Line of Fire

Phoenix Yard, 2014   ISBN: 9781907912399

When illustrator Barroux found a cardboard box in a skip near his Paris home, he had no idea what it might contain. What he found was an old notebook, which turned out to be the diary of a soldier, describing his experiences in the early months of the First World War. With Barroux's illustrations, the diary became *On Les Aura*, published in English in Sarah Ardizzone's translation as *Line of Fire*. It's a raw, unfussy depiction of the desolate world in which these soldiers were fighting, written with no literary pretensions and all the more powerful for that. **12+**

BESSORA

Translated from the French by Sarah Ardizzone. Illustrated by Barroux

Alpha

The Bucket List, 2016   ISBN: 9781911370017

Novelist Bessora was awarded the Fénéon Prize in 2001 and the Grand prix littéraire d'Afrique noire in 2007. Her protagonist here, Alpha Coulibaly, is emblematic of the refugee crisis today – just one of millions on the move, at the mercy of people traffickers, endlessly frustrated, endangered and exploited as he attempts to rejoin his family, already in Europe. The book is presented in graphic novel format, with artwork created by Barroux in cheap felt-tip pen and wash, materials Alpha himself might be able to access. This timely and important account of one man's desperate journey comes to the UK market with a foreword by Michael Morpurgo, and is supported by Amnesty International and English PEN. **12+**

> I was blown away by *Alpha*, a searing graphic novel about one man's desperate and dangerous journey from an intolerable life in the Ivory Coast to reach France and his family. The sparing, powerful text, fantastically translated into vernacular English, is perfectly complemented by compelling illustrations. Together they provide a devastating and important insight into the plight of refugees.
>
> —Anne Harding, independent trainer

BSHARAT, AHLAM

Translated from the Arabic by Nancy Roberts

Code Name: Butterfly

Neem Tree Press, 2016 ISBN: 9781911107026

Bsharat is a Palestinian writer, and in *Code Name: Butterfly* she conjures up a teenage girl living under the Israeli occupation. In some ways 'Butterfly' (not her real name) is just like any other teenager, complex and dramatic, with many of the same preoccupations (friendship, rivalry, family tensions, impossible dreams), but the harsh political and social conditions in which she lives are quite unlike anything most of the book's readers will recognise. Enlightening, funny and affecting, *Code Name: Butterfly* is a brief story that packs quite a punch. **12+**

CHOTJEWITZ, DAVID

Translated from the German by Doris Orgel

Daniel Half Human

Simon & Schuster, 2006 ISBN: 9780689857485

From a German writer and theatre director this book provides an interestingly different perspective on the persecution of the Jews in Germany. Daniel believes himself to be Aryan and is all set to join his best friend Armin in becoming an active member of the Hitler Youth, but then he finds out that his mother is Jewish, making him half Jewish and therefore half human in the eyes of the 'supreme' Aryan race. Soon he and Armin find themselves set against each other – and, as World War II progresses, each holds the other's life in their hands. This is a tense and thought-provoking story of racism and friendship in the aftermath of Kristallnacht and an important contribution to anti-Semitism and Second World War literature for adolescents. **12+**

D'ADAMO, FRANCESCO

Translated from the Italian by Siân Williams

Oh, Freedom!

Darf Publishing, 2016 ISBN: 9781850772859

The story of the American 'underground railroad', the network that helped nineteenth-century slaves to escape to places where they could be free, is an important and inspiring one. We discover it here through the story of ten-year-old Tommy and his family, who brave countless dangers to follow banjo-playing Peg Leg Joe on the journey from the Alabama plantation where they are enslaved, to a new life. There's plenty of atmospheric historical detail (though never enough to swamp the story), there's excitement galore and a potent, timely message. Some historical stories, even if they're set a hundred and fifty years ago, still resonate powerfully in today's world – this is unquestionably one of them. **12+**

DALAGER, STIG

Translated from the Danish by Frances Osterfelt and Cheryl Robson

David's Story

Aurora Metro Publications, 2010 ISBN: 9781906582043

One of Denmark's most distinguished authors writing for children and adults, Dalager based this novel upon the accounts and diaries of Jewish children from this horrific period of World War Two in Poland. Written with great simplicity, mostly in the first person, it tells a story which begins with the start of restrictions on Jewish life, and advances to roundups, forced marches, the ghetto and transportation. This is a moving and vivid addition to literature of the Holocaust. **12+**

DE FOMBELLE, TIMOTHÉE

Translated from the French by Sarah Ardizzone and Sam Gordon

The Book of Pearl

Walker, 2016　　　　ISBN: 9781406364620

A beautifully written, timeless tale of heroic love, which seamlessly weaves a fantasy mystery within the historical setting of France in World War II. Joshua Pearl is from a world that our own no longer believes in. He knows that his great love is waiting for him in that distant place, but he is trapped in our time. As his memories begin to fade, he discovers strange objects, tiny fragments of a story from a long time ago. Can Joshua remember the past and believe in his own story before his love is lost forever? **12+**

> Walker Books' long tradition of publishing books in translation comes quite simply from our desire to publish the finest authors and the best books, wherever they come from. We're as proud of Timothée de Fombelle and Cao Wenxuan as we are of Patrick Ness and David Almond. De Fombelle's latest YA masterpiece, *The Book of Pearl*, which fuses reality and fairy tale in a search for lost love, firmly establishes him as one of the best writers anywhere in the world.
>
> —Jane Winterbotham, publisher

DE FOMBELLE, TIMOTHÉE

Translated from the French by Sarah Ardizzone

Vango: Between Sky and Earth

Walker, 2013　　　　ISBN: 9781406354010

Shipwrecked and then raised in Sicily by Mademoiselle, his slightly strange nanny, Vango grows up with just one friend, the priest Zefiro, who lives in a monastery hidden from sight. Vango decides to follow Zefiro into holy orders, but at the moment he is taking his vows at Notre Dame in Paris, he is falsely accused of a crime and has to go on the run. This is a breathless and highly cinematic story that follows Vango travelling by Zeppelin across Europe from Stromboli to Nazi Germany, from Scotland to the Soviet Union, climbing the rooftops of Paris, crossing the paths of arms traffickers, crooked policemen, Russian spies and even Stalin. Timothée de Fombelle is an incredible storyteller and has created such an intricate tale of intrigue and adventure with such compelling characters that readers will devour this book and its sequel, *Vango: A Prince without a Kingdom* (ISBN: 9781406360028). **12+**

DUMAS, ALEXANDRE

Translated from the French by Richard Pevear

The Three Musketeers

Penguin Classics, 2008　　　　ISBN: 9780141442341

One of the most widely read of French authors and translated into over 100 languages, Dumas specialises in historical adventures of which this is probably the best known. *The Three Musketeers* was one of three novels in his D'Artagnan Romances, the others being *Twenty Years After* and *The Vicomte of Bragelonne: Ten Years Later*. Innumerable film and media adaptations are testament to the enduring appeal of this tale of the brave and noble musketeers enmeshed in the struggle between the evil Cardinal Richelieu and the king and their own doomed love stories. **12+**

FRANK, ANNE (EDITED BY OTTO H. FRANK AND MIRJAM PRESSLER)

Translated from the Dutch by Susan Massotty

The Diary of a Young Girl

Penguin, 2012 ISBN: 9780241952436

The Dutch-language diary kept by Anne Frank while she was in hiding for two years with her family during the Nazi occupation of the Netherlands really needs no introduction, but remains one of the most important works ever to be translated into English. The family was apprehended in 1944, and Anne Frank died of typhus in the Bergen-Belsen concentration camp, but the diary was retrieved by Miep Gies, who gave it to Anne's father, Otto Frank, the family's only known survivor, just after the war was over. The diary has since been published in more than 60 languages. Young readers can really engage and empathise with Anne because she is a normal teen, thinking at least as much about friends, and boyfriends, and how her parents annoy her, as she does about issues of the day. She is a remarkably clever, thoughtful narrator, and her diary is as entertaining as it is a significant historical document. **12+**

FUNKE, CORNELIA

Translated from the German by Oliver Latsch

The Thief Lord

Chicken House, 2006 ISBN: 9781905294213

Desperate to avoid being separated after the death of their parents, Prosper and Bo run away to Venice, the city of their imagination. It is all rather different until they meet the little band of displaced children living in the abandoned cinema under the protection of the Thief Lord. But who is he really? And what is the mystery hidden on Secret Island? *The Thief Lord* combines the realism of an exciting adventure, a mystery to solve and a villain to outwit with an intriguing fantasy, all hallmarks of this increasingly accomplished author. This was the first of Funke's novels to appear in English and countless others treats have followed. **12+**

GEDA, FABIO

Translated from the Italian by Howard Curtis

In the Sea there are Crocodiles

Tamarind, 2015 ISBN: 9781848531383

In a book that takes a true story and shapes it into a beautiful piece of fiction, Italian novelist Fabio Geda describes Enaiatollah's remarkable journey from Afghanistan to Italy where he finally managed to claim political asylum aged fifteen and where he met Fabio Geda, with whom he became friends. In Geda's hands, Enaiatollah's journey becomes a universal story of stoicism in the face of fear, and the search for a place where life is liveable. **12+**

Aged only ten, Enaiatollah Akbari was left by his mother and had to make his way alone from Afghanistan to Italy and safety. The journey took five years. This heart-breaking and riveting story, beautifully written and translated, is a testament to the power of the human spirit. Now translated into 28 languages, and with over 400,000 copies sold, it's a powerful record of what young asylum-seekers have to endure. The book deservedly won the UK Marsh Award for Children's Literature in Translation and a film is now in the pipeline. Enaiatollah asked author Fabio Geda to write it so that people who had suffered similar things could know that they were not alone, and that others might understand them better. A book indeed for our times.   —Siân Williams, director, Children's Book Show

MANKELL, HENNING

Translated from the Swedish by Laurie Thompson

A Bridge to the Stars

Andersen Press, 2005   ISBN: 9781842704394

This novel is a coming-of-age tale set during the cold, dark winter nights of Northern Sweden and the descriptions of the frozen landscape are in striking contrast to the warmth of emotion that erupts between father and son. This is the first of four books on the life of Joel Gustafsson. Joel is eleven and lives with his father Samuel after Jenny his mum left them. The story is loosely autobiographical, based on the author's own experience of being brought up by his father. Joel is desperate to find out why his Mother left and becomes fascinated by the nocturnal activities of his neighbours – 'mad' Simon Windstorm and 'No-Nose' Gertrud – and his encounter with the strange boy, Ture, with whom he builds an uneasy friendship as they plan their 'Secret Society'. Joel discovers considerably more than he ever expected, which helps him to understand his own family, and himself. Joel's story continues in *Shadows in the Twilight*, *When the Snow Fell* and *The Journey to the End of the World*. **12+**

MANKELL, HENNING

Translated from the Swedish by Anne Connie Stuksrud

Secrets in the Fire

Allen & Unwin, 2000   ISBN: 9781865081816

Swedish author Henning Mankell is best known for his Wallander detective novels, but he also lived part of each year in Africa, and this important book is based on a true story of an indomitable young girl living in war-torn Mozambique. In beautifully spare, unsentimental language he tells the story of Sofia's shattered childhood and how she is forced to rebuild her life when she and her sister, Maria, are involved in a landmine explosion that has devastating consequences – her sister is killed and she loses both her legs. Pitted against incredible adversity Sofia's courage manages to shine through as she comes to terms with her terrible disability and her life transcends the brutal futility and horror of war. **12+**

PULLMAN, PHILIP AND MELCHIOR, STÉPHANE (ADAPTER)

Translated from the French by Philip Pullman and Annie Eaton. Illustrated by Clément Oubrerie

Northern Lights: The Graphic Novel

Doubleday, 2015   ISBN: 9780857534620

Philip Pullman's incredible *Northern Lights* is not a translation, of course; but curiously this version is. As an example of the way great stories travel, Pullman's novel was made into this graphic novel in France, and only later was translated from the French to find its way back into the English market. Some of the complexity of the novel is inevitably lost in the interest of clear lively narrative, but a great deal remains, too; a thrillingly paced plot here only enhanced by stunning visuals. **12+**

SATRAPI, MARJANE

Translated from the French by Mattias Ripa (part 1) and Blake Ferris (part 2)

Persepolis: The Story of an Iranian Childhood (Parts 1 and 2)

Jonathan Cape, 2003   ISBN: 9780224064408

The two *Persepolis* books use the graphic novel form to tell the story of ten-year-old Marji (a version of Satrapi herself) and her family in Iran, in the years immediately following the Islamic revolution. We see her childhood idealism, her rebellion, the strength of her bonds with her family (her grandmother in particular) and the war-torn climate in which everyone is trying to survive. In the second volume, we follow her years as a student in Vienna, including a return visit to Tehran, right up to her early adulthood. Together the two volumes make up a frank and engaging story, and the perfect introduction to lives like Marji's and the world she comes from; and Satrapi's densely inked artwork is bold and appealing. The visual style was recreated in the – also excellent – animated film adaptation. **12+**

TAKEUCHI, NAOKO

Translated from the Japanese by William Flanagan (volumes 1–8) and Mari Maramoto (volumes 9–12)

Sailor Moon (volumes 1–12)

Kodansha, 2011 ISBN: 9781935429746 (volume 1)

Sailor Moon has received wide critical acclaim and has become one of the most popular manga and anime series worldwide. The entire series has sold over 35 million copies, making it one of the highest selling shōjo series ever, and reviewers have praised the art, characterization and humour of the story. The anime series is popular in several countries and is arguably one of the most influential in boosting the popularity of Japanese animation in Western culture. **12+**

> While manga has a rich, complex history, the one example that made this form of comics and its visual style particularly successful in the English-speaking world came in Naoko Takeuchi's 'magical girl' series – or mahou shōjo, comics aimed at young female readers, featuring characters who use magic and a focus on relationships – *Sailor Moon*. Schoolgirl Usagi Tsukino can transform into a fighter for justice, along with a team of other astronomically-named Sailor Guardians, thanks to the powers of a magic crystal. The fighting is only a corollary to the exploration of female friendship, LGBT+ and other romantic relationships, and regular teenage issues in Japanese society.
> —Alex Valente, comics translation expert

VAN KOOIJ, RACHEL

Translated from the German by Siobhan Parkinson

Bartolomé: The Infanta's Pet

Little Island, 2012 ISBN: 9781908195265

This highly memorable novel was inspired by a real painting, 'Las Meninas' by Velásquez, on display in the Museo del Prado in Madrid, and is truly international: written in German by a Dutch Austrian, set in Spain, translated into English and published in Ireland. Seventeenth-century Madrid is not a kind place for a child like Bartolomé. He has restricted growth, deformed feet and kyphosis (curvature of the upper back, then known as a 'hunch back') and his family keep him hidden in a small back room. Then the King's little daughter, the Infanta, wants to have him as her 'human-dog'. But life in the royal palace is scary, cruel and humiliating until Bartolomé discovers solace and comfort in the artist's studio. Colourful, gripping, and written with real warmth, this is an inspiring story of courage and hope. Van Kooij's beautiful prose brings us into Bartolomé's life and, through his eyes, she writes about how being different ultimately makes an already strong boy even stronger. **12+**

VERNE, JULES

Translated from the French by William Butcher

Twenty Thousand Leagues under the Seas

Oxford World Classics, 2009   ISBN: 9780199539277

Despite the common perception, the title of this classic French adventure actually refers to the distance travelled while under the sea and not to a depth, as 20,000 leagues is over six times the diameter, and nearly three times the circumference of the Earth. Originally serialized from March 1869 through to June 1870 in the *Magasin d'Éducation et de Récréation,* this is considered to be one of Verne's greatest works and one which stands up to scientific progress slightly more than *Journey to the Centre of the Earth,* for example. Fantastically exciting set-pieces abound, including a submarine hunting expedition, a tour of Atlantis and an attack from a group of giant squids. Another of its strengths is the character of Captain Nemo himself, a memorably tortured character who is both impeccable host and sinister jailor. **12+**

> When I first started working in children's book publishing I harboured a secret that I was sure would get me fired: the child me didn't like (most) children's fiction. I was a vivacious reader of non-fiction but for more than a couple of years the only fiction that wasn't a chore or came anywhere close to delivering the same other-worldly adventures in outer space or the plot twists and characters in ancient history were Jules Verne's science fiction novels. The possibility that these novels existed – let alone started life – in another language never crossed my mind. Until, that is, I had to move to France aged 13. After the humiliation of mispronouncing the author's name in front of my new peers, came the grudging acceptance that I needed to learn to read my favourite books again. Beneath the surface of what seemed like impenetrable foreignness lay a comforting familiarity that was worth the grind. *Vingt mille lieues sous les mers* – *Twenty Thousand Leagues under the Sea* – was the first whole book I read in French.
>
> —Emma Langley, Arts Council England

WENXUAN, CAO

Translated from the Chinese by Helen Wang

Bronze and Sunflower

Walker, 2015   ISBN: 9781406348460

The author is a Professor of Chinese literature at Peking University and became the first Chinese author to win the Hans Christian Andersen Award for children's literature in 2016, which is highly appropriate for an author deemed China's own Hans Andersen! Set in rural China in the late 1960s and early 1970s at the time of the Cultural Revolution this is the story of Sunflower, the daughter of an artist banished to do hard labour at a rural cadre school, and Bronze, the mute son of impoverished villagers who live nearby. After Sunflower's father dies, Bronze persuades his parents to take her in and the family devotes itself to giving her a decent life in the face of the extreme hardship that threatens repeatedly to destroy them. This is a story that is beautifully written, evocative, and harrowing, but ultimately truly heart-warming. **12+**

WYSS, JOHANN DAVID

Translated from the German by William Godwin

The Swiss Family Robinson

Puffin, 2009 ISBN: 9780141325309

Like the narrator of this classic story, the author was a Swiss pastor who had four sons. Said to be inspired by Daniel Defoe's *Robinson Crusoe* and now an international classic bestseller with numerous film and TV adaptations and a science fiction spoof to its credit, this tale portrays a family's struggle to create a new life for themselves on a strange and fantastic tropical island. One needs to allow a certain amount of poetic licence as the island contains hundreds of animals and plants not normally seen together, but it is the authenticity of the boys' behaviour and the ingenuity of the family that ensures this remains one of the world's best-loved and most enduring stories of shipwreck and survival. **12+**

ZAFÓN, CARLOS RUIZ

Translated from the Spanish by Lucia Graves

The Midnight Palace

Orion, 2012 ISBN: 9780753829240

From the Spanish author of the phenomenally successful adult novel *Shadow of the Wind*, this novel proves that he can write just as effectively for young adults. It's a page-turning supernatural thriller, with a cast of memorable characters, that begins in 1916 with a British army Lieutenant Michael Peake being chased through the dark streets of Calcutta. His life is in imminent danger because he harbours a secret; beneath his coat are two new-born babies who must be saved at all costs. Sixteen years later Ben and his friends are preparing to leave the orphanage where they have grown up. They have formed a secret club, The Chowbar Society, which meets each week in a derelict mansion they have christened The Midnight Palace. But an old woman stops them. She introduces Ben to Sheere, the sister from whom he was separated at birth. She tells them about their past – of an accident, a ghostly railway station, a bird of fire, and the curse that threatens to destroy their future. **12+**

14+

AMBROSIO, GABRIELLA
Translated from the Italian by Alistair McEwen
Before We Say Goodbye
Walker, 2010   ISBN: 9781406325041

Set in Jerusalem in 2002, the drama takes place during a single day. Each short chapter covers an hour in the day starting at 7.00am in the morning. It follows the characters as they go about their daily lives revealing their thoughts, feelings and experiences of living in Jerusalem. As each hour passes the tension mounts building up to a horrendous climax of a suicide bombing, which poignantly is based on the true story of the Kiryat HaYovel supermarket bombing in Jerusalem, committed by Ayat al-Akhras, a seventeen-year-old Palestinian girl from the Dheisheh refugee camp. What makes this Italian author's debut novel so special is that it does not take sides; there is no bias and no judgement. It has become a set textbook in Italian secondary schools and Amnesty International funded its translation into both Hebrew and Arabic. It has since been adopted by schools, colleges and human rights organisations working in this troubled region. **14+**

COHEN-SCALI, SARAH
Translated from the French by Penny Hueston
Max
Walker, 2016   ISBN: 9781406368253

Winner of the prestigious Prix Sorcières and endorsed by Amnesty International, this is a hard and harrowing read. Baby Max is the perfect prototype for the Nazi eugenics programme; he is the ideal size, he has the correct colour hair and flawless blue eyes and was born on Hitler's birthday. This brilliantly written story captures the horrific reality of Nazism through the eyes of an anything but innocent child and yet allows you to feel empathy even towards him. **16+**

> This 'memoir' of a child born into the Lebensborn (Nazi eugenics) programme is visceral, brutal and utterly, breathtakingly brilliant. As hard to put down as it is to stomach, this highly perceptive novel quietly yet emphatically shifts the ground beneath your feet, asking morally complex and scarily relevant questions about both victims and perpetrators of evil. Intense, urgent, and audacious, be prepared for *Max* to leave you breathless, devastated and yet utterly dazzled by Cohen-Scali's taut, terrifying and very clever storytelling.
>
> —Zoe Toft, Playing By The Book

DE VELASCO, STEFANIE

Translated from the German by Tim Mohr

Tiger Milk

Head of Zeus, 2014 ISBN: 9781781857441

Unsurprisingly, many books with teenage protagonists are about growing up. But in *Tiger Milk* the two central teenage girls do an awful lot of growing up very quickly indeed. Nini and Jameelah are fourteen, and impatient to be adults, so over the course of a summer they do what they can to experience all manner of new things – all the usual kinds of rebellion, and them some… Though uncompromising, unsentimental, and sometimes shocking, *Tiger Milk* is really driven by Nini's voice – which makes it hard to put down – and the girls' evolving friendship against a gritty Berlin backdrop. **14+**

DE VIGAN, DELPHINE

Translated from the French by George Miller

No and Me

Bloomsbury, 2010 ISBN: 9780747599647

Thirteen-year-old Parisian girl Lou Bertignac is very precocious indeed, but the last thing she wants to do is to give a presentation in front of her whole class, having them all looking at her… But then watching people at Austerlitz station, Lou strikes up a conversation with eighteen-year-old No, who is pretty in spite of the dirt and her missing tooth, and homeless. Lou chooses the plight of the homeless as the subject for her class presentation, and No will be her interviewee. And then No takes up temporary residence with Lou's imperfect family, with dramatic effects on all concerned. With moments of tenderness and truth about family and home, about inadequate parents and neglected children, *No and Me* is honest but also at least partially reassuring; Lou's 'experiment against fate' might not go quite according to plan, but de Vigan shows that things really can change. **14+**

FETH, MONIKA

Translated from the German by Anthea Bell

The Strawberry Picker

Definitions, 2007 ISBN: 9780099488460

An ex-journalist, Feth has written an incredibly tense psychological thriller which plays cat and mouse with the reader's emotions. Eighteen-year-old Jenna is sharing a flat in Bröhl, Germany, with her friends Caro and Merle when a girl is killed nearby. The murder seems to have parallels with two other frightening crimes. Then one day Caro is found murdered – stabbed seven times and with her necklace missing, just like the other girls. At the funeral Jenna swears revenge in front of everybody, and in turn attracts the attention of Nat, a handsome and mysterious strawberry picker. There is no mystery about the identity of the killer, Feth is more interested in the aftermath of a murder, how it affects loved ones and how people cope with the trauma of losing someone in such a brutal way. **16+**

GAARDER, JOSTEIN
Translated from the Norwegian by Paulette Møller
Sophie's World
Orion, 2003   ISBN: 9781858815305

Sophie's World became a surprise hit when it appeared in English in 1995, and not just among teen readers. A surprise because it's essentially a history of western philosophical thought, which is not the kind of subject that frequently troubles the bestseller lists. But this one is brilliantly conceived – it introduces us to one teenage girl, the eponymous Sophie, and as she learns about philosophy (from a mysterious philosopher called Alberto Knox with whom she corresponds), we readers learn, too. But it isn't quite as simple as that, since before we know it, our (and Sophie's) very understanding of reality is being challenged… Complex, gripping and truly unique. **14+**

> When I was only thirteen or fourteen, I discovered *Sophie's World* by Jostein Gaarder. I was blessed with a wonderful English teacher who revelled in suggesting new authors, even loaning me gems from her own shelves. This was one of her first recommendations. It fired my imagination, sparking a powerful new interest in philosophy. It was like nothing I had encountered – extraordinary, unpredictable, thought-provoking, raising fundamental questions about the very nature of our existence, challenging me both as a reader and a thinker. I haven't revisited it in adulthood, for fear that any of its strange magic might have faded.
> —Alexandra Strick, Outside In World

GUÈNE, FAÏZA
Translated from the French by Sarah Ardizzone
Just Like Tomorrow
Definitions, 2006   ISBN: 9781862301580

Just Like Tomorrow gives us a year in the life of Doria, a fifteen year old living in Paradise, the ironically named estate in the Paris banlieues. Doria is first-generation French, the daughter to North African immigrants, and life for her community is vibrant but never easy. Doria herself is excellent company – sharp, drily funny and perceptive. In her memorable streetwise voice (every bit as contemporary and urban in Sarah Ardizzone's south London recreation), she shares her observations about those around her, and about her life in an often hostile society; and we watch her develop and grow in confidence as she does. (And if you like this, be sure not to miss Guène/Ardizzone's *Dreams from the Endz*, too.) **14+**

HANIKA, BEATE TERESA
Translated from the German by Katy Derbyshire
Learning to Scream
Andersen Press, 2010   ISBN: 9781849390606

This is a disturbing first-person narrative about a teenage girl sexually abused by her grandfather since early childhood. As she gradually faces the detail of these past events she discovers the strength to move on, and form new relationships. Heart-breaking and emotional, the very powerful, clear, poetic writing handles a difficult topic with sensitivity and the detail is never gratuitous or sensational. As you turn the pages you are desperate for Malvina to tell someone. Some of the passages towards the end of the novel are unbearably moving, particularly when Malvina finally tells Lizzy what she has endured. From the beginning the readers' sympathy and understanding are engaged in this ultimately uplifting story of triumph over evil. **16+**

HERRNDORF, WOLFGANG

Translated from the German by Tim Mohr

Why We Took the Car

Andersen Press, 2014   ISBN: 9781783440313

Why We Took the Car is the story of a road trip like no other. School misfit Mike is bracing himself for a bad summer holiday, when his new Russian classmate appears with a 'borrowed' car, and their unlikely ride begins. Their sometimes pleasingly surreal adventures take them all over the country, meeting interesting people and new challenges, and learning something about the world, friendship and themselves along the way. Narrator Mike and his new friend are beautifully drawn characters, and their coming-of-age story is funny and full of psychological insight and warmth. **15+**

HOFFMANN, E.T.A.

Translated from the German by R.J. Hollindale

Tales of Hoffmann

Penguin Classic, 1982   ISBN: 9780140443929

These tales form the basis of Offenbach's famous opera of the same name. Hoffmann's stories were very influential during the 19th century, and he is one of the major authors of the Romantic movement. This selection of Hoffmann's finest short stories vividly demonstrates his intense imagination and preoccupation with the supernatural, placing him at the forefront of both surrealism and the modern horror genre. Master of the bizarre, Hoffmann creates a sinister and unsettling world combining love and madness, black humour and bewildering illusion.**14+**

JANSEN, HANNA

Translated from the German by Elizabeth D. Crawford

Over a Thousand Hills I Walk with You

Andersen Press, 2007   ISBN: 9781842706732

This sometimes brutal story of Jeanne d'Arc Umubyeyi, a girl caught up in the 1994 Rwanda genocide, is told as a novel, and reads like one; but in fact it's based on reality, for Jeanne d'Arc is herself the German author's adopted daughter. From which you can deduce that, yes, she does escape to Europe, and yes, it does end well, but it takes many harrowing experiences to get there. This brave and powerful book isn't afraid to deal with Jeanne d'Arc's most distressing losses, and some horrific cruelty, but it's ultimately an inspiring read, if not an easy one. **14+**

MEYER, KAI

Translated from the German by Anthea Bell

Arcadia Awakens

Templar, 2012   ISBN: 9781848776319

Kai Meyer is the author of many highly acclaimed and popular books for adults and young adults in his native Germany. Here we have paranormal fantasy with a twist: *Romeo and Juliet* meets shape-shifting Mafia families in the first book of an exciting trilogy. As well as the realistic detail of the Mafia, with the treachery, crime, violence, cruelty and deceit of the Cosa Nostra, we have the evocative Sicilian countryside and the ancient myth of a civilisation of shape-shifters. A fantastic, action-packed, suspenseful book that is sure to keep readers on edge from page to page. **14+**

MURAIL, MARIE-AUDE

Translated from the French by Adriana Hunter

My Brother Simple

Bloomsbury, 2012   ISBN: 9781408814710

Funny, thought-provoking and clever, this French bestseller won the Prix SNCF du Livre de Jeunesse and was dramatised for French television; in Germany it won the prestigious Deutscher Jugendliteraturpreis. This highly original tale is an unforgettable story of a boy with learning difficulties who brings profound changes to the lives of four Parisian student flat sharers and to his own seventeen-year-old brother, Kleber, who refuses to let their father put Simple into an institution. We can all learn from Simple's way of looking at the world: his enviable levels of logic, his honesty and humour and the way he peels away the superficial layers the other characters hide behind. It is utterly joyous, moving and life-affirming. **16+**

OESTERHELD, HÉCTOR GÉRMAN

Translated from the Spanish by Erica Mena. Illustrated by Francisco Solano López

The Eternaut

Fantagraphics Books, 2015   ISBN: 9781606998502

Oesterheld's sci-fi comic first appeared in serialised form way back in the fifties, and has been revived at various times since (with a changing roster of writers following Oesterheld's disappearance in 1977), but it has only very lately been translated into English. It begins with a deadly blizzard in Buenos Aires that turns out to have been caused by an alien invasion, and goes on to recount the attempts of Juan Salvo and his family and friends – all of them ordinary people forced by circumstances to be resourceful and heroic – to survive and defeat the invading forces. While *The Eternaut* can of course be read just for the thrills of the plot and the detailed lines of Solano López's art, there are many more layers for interested readers to discover, not least what seems like quite bold political commentary, written as it was in a military-led Argentina. **16+**

SALVI, MANUELA

Translated from the Italian by Denise Muir

Girl Detached

The Bucket List, 2016   ISBN: 9781911370024

After this and a picture book were banned in her native Italy the author came to the UK to study censorship. Luckily this book was picked up by a UK publisher because it is a powerful novel dealing with a very important topic: the grooming and sexual exploitation of teenage girls. The vulnerable Aleksandra is painfully shy and when her grandmother's death forces her to move in with the mother she thinks abandoned her as a baby, she meets the charismatic, confident Megan and begins to take on a new persona. She is introduced to Ruben, and gradually they begin what she thinks is a relationship. However, her new group isn't what it seems and things begin to spiral massively out of control. Horrifyingly realistic and tense, shocking in its detail but without being gratuitous, this is uncomfortable but essential reading. **16+**

SIMUKKA, SALLA
Translated from the Finnish by Owen F. Witesman
As Red as Blood
Hot Key, 2014   ISBN: 9781471402463

The first in Salla Simukka's gripping series opens with a landscape of clean white snow, except that Natalia Smirnova is lying face down in it and she has been shot dead and the white snow is slowly turning blood-red… This is a story of crime and danger, with a terrific heroine at its heart – Lumikki Andersson, a bright, strong, independent high school student who never expected to get mixed up in such things… There are another two equally atmospheric thrillers in the so-called 'Snow White Trilogy': *As White as Snow* and *As Black as Ebony*. **15+**

TELLER, JANNE
Translated from the Danish by Martin Aitken
Nothing
Strident, 2011   ISBN: 9781905537389

I'm guessing you probably haven't ever read a nihilist Danish YA novel before? Well, you've been missing out. Janne Teller's brilliant and fearless story asks the biggest of existential questions: what's the meaning of life? Thirteen-year-old Pierre-Anthon has decided it is just meaningless, and so he has climbed a tree with no intention of coming back down; so it falls to his friends to try and coax him down with evidence that, yes, life really does matter. But be warned: you'd do well not to expect something reassuring or sentimental – what happens as the story plays out is dark (there are echoes of *Lord of the Flies*, among others) and profoundly unsettling… **15+**

TURTSCHANINOFF, MARIA
Translated from the Swedish by A.A. Prime
Maresi (The Red Abbey Chronicles)
Pushkin Children's Books, 2016   ISBN: 9781782690917

A startlingly unusual and original novel from Finland. The setting is an island in an unspecified fantasy world inhabited by a community of women who live separate from men, dedicating themselves to the worship of the Triple Goddess. Maresi is a young novice, sent there by her family to escape famine, and still wracked by guilt over the death of her little sister. She loves her new life, the women live austere lives but there's ample time for friendship and study. Their peace is threatened when another girl arrives, on the run from her violent father, and the reader quickly realises that he will never let his daughter escape. The tension before his arrival is palpable, and the violence he brings with him is truly shocking. Even so, he's no match for Maresi! This strongly feminist parable of sisterhood and bravery will enthral readers. **14+**

VAN LIESHOUT, TED
Translated from the Dutch by Lance Salway
Brothers
Collins Flamingo, 2001   ISBN: 9780007112319

A short, but nevertheless incredibly powerful, novel that won the prestigious Deutscher Jugendliteraturpreis in 1999. The Dutch author is renowned for pushing the boundaries of children's literature and this semi-autobiographical book tackles head-on a number of tricky subjects such as death, sexuality and family relationships. Luke is trying to come to terms with the death of his brother and, while reading his brother's diary, he not only discovers that his brother was gay, but comes to realise that he himself is also. The reader is engaged instantly through the novel's intimate narrative diary format and superb characterisation. **14+**

ZENATTI, VALÉRIE

Translated from the French by Adriana Hunter

When I Was a Soldier

Bloomsbury, 2005   ISBN: 9780747575665

This is a fascinating true story of a young girl's experience of her two years' national service in the Israeli Defence Army (IDF). Born and raised in France, Zenatti emigrated to Israel when she was thirteen, and subsequently experienced Israeli service at eighteen, as a relative outsider. She returned to France and wrote about these experiences in French maintaining that external perspective on the experience. This is a perceptive novel that paints an illuminating portrait of a young woman growing up in a society where violent conflict is accepted as part of everyday normal life. **14+**

Riveting Reads: A World of Books in Translation

Beyond this...

It will not have escaped your attention that despite our very best endeavours there are still all too few books to share from the wider world beyond Europe, and most especially from Africa and Asia.

This important initiative may help to change that situation:

In Other Words is a new project to promote the translation and UK publication of outstanding children's literature from around the world. BookTrust will sponsor sample translations from 10 children's books, which have not previously been published in the English language. The selected translations will be presented to the UK publishing community at the Bologna Book Fair in April 2017. Four of these titles will be selected as specially commended 'Honour titles'. All 10 titles will be available for British publishers to purchase from the rights holders. Titles that are purchased by British publishers will be supported by a £1,500 grant towards marketing and publicity. Selection and judging will be carried out by a panel of experts, including top children's translators and children's book experts. In Other Words is funded by Arts Council England http://www.booktrust.org.uk/prizes/23.

Let us hope that this, together with the changes to the CILIP Carnegie medal criteria which now allow the first English translation of a novel published in the UK to be eligible for the medal that all publishers want to win, will generate a more positive and welcoming environment for children's literature in translation from all around the world.

In order to keep up with what becomes available, other than through the review pages of *The School Librarian, Books for Keeps, Carousel* and from the pitifully little review coverage provided in the mainstream press, you can check the following specific sources of information:

Outside In World

An organisation dedicated to promoting and exploring world literature and children's books in translation. Outside In World was set up in 2007 as a not-for-profit organisation. On the website you find a wealth of information about books, authors, illustrators, projects and useful resources. The site allows you to search for books in various different ways – by age range or by continent/country or by author, title or keyword http://www.outsideinworld.org.uk

Marsh Award for Children's Literature in Translation

The Award is presented biennially and recognises the best translation into English of a children's book published within the previous two years. The purpose of the Award is to celebrate the best translation of a children's book from a foreign language into English, thereby promoting children's literature across different cultures, making great stories more accessible to young readers. It also highlights the important role of the translator, who can often be overlooked.
http://www.marshchristiantrust.org/Childrens_Literature_Translation

2016 saw the launch of the My Marsh video review competition for schools, based upon the shortlisted titles announced in October 2016. http://www.esu.org/our-work/english-translation-awards

Chinese Books for Young Readers

Set up by an international group of three – Helen Wang (based in the UK), Anna Gustafsson Chen (based in Sweden) and Minjie Chen (based in the USA) who read Chinese books for young people, in Chinese and English – the new website and blog will provide information about Chinese books for children.
https://chinesebooksforyoungreaders.wordpress.com/

IBBY UK
IBBY UK is the British section of the International Board on Books for Young People. IBBY was founded in 1953 in Zurich, Switzerland as an international network which acts as a forum for people working in all areas connected with children's books and reading. It is responsible for the Hans Christian Andersen Awards, maintains the IBBY documentation centre for disabled young people, compiles biennial IBBY honour lists of outstanding children's books published in member countries, publishes *Bookbird*, organises a biennial International Congress, and is committed to supporting the growth of children's literature and literacy in developing countries.
http://www.ibby.org.uk

Publishers

Whilst major publishers, most notably those such as Andersen Press, Bloomsbury and Walker, do publish occasional books in translation, these smaller presses concentrate upon this area.

Alma Books
Hogarth House, 32-34 Paradise Road, Richmond, Surrey, TW9 1SE
Tel: 020 8940 6917   http://www.almabooks.com

Aurora Metro Books
67 Grove Avenue, Twickenham, TW1 4HX
Tel: 020 3261 0000   http://www.aurorametro.com

Book Island
42 Thornleigh Road, Bristol BS7 8PH
info@bookisland.co.uk   www.bookisland.co.uk

Cinebook: The 9th Art Publishers
56 Beech Avenue. Chartham, Canterbury, Kent CT4 7TA
Tel: 01227 731 368   http://www.cinebook.co.uk/about_us.php
Publisher of the best-selling European comic books for all ages in English

Gecko Press
PO Box 9335, Marion Square, Wellington, 6141, New Zealand
Tel: +64 (0) 4 801 9333   http://www.geckopress.com
(Distributed in the UK by Bounce Marketing)

Pushkin Children's Books
Pushkin Press, 124-128 Barlby Road, London W10 6BL
Tel: 020 7470 8830   http://pushkinchildrens.com

Tiny Owl Publishing
1 Repton House, London, SW1V 2LD
info@tinyowl.co.uk   http://tinyowl.co.uk

Index of Authors

Aakeson, Kim Fupz 21	Hergé.....................28	Schmidt, Annie M.G. 38
Acioli, Socorro 41	Herrndorf, Wolfgang 52	Sepúlveda, Luis 38
Alemagna, Beatrice 9	Hoffmann. E.T.A. 52	Simukka, Salla.....................54
Ambrosio, Gabrielle 49	Hoffmann, Heinrich 12	Spyri, Johanna 39
Atxaga, Bernardo 21	Holm, Anne 28	Stark, Ulf.....................15
Aubry, Cécile 21	Holzwarth, Werner.....................13	Starobinets, Anna 39
Baisch, Milena.....................22	Hub, Ulrich 28	Steinhöfel, Andreas 39
Barroux 9,41	Hwang, Sun-mi.....................29	Strid, Jakob Martin 15
Bauer, Jutta 9	Inui, Tomiko 29	Taghdis, Susan 16
Behrangi, Samad 10	Janosch.....................13	Takeuchi, Naoko.....................46
Berna, Paul 22	Jansen, Hanna.....................52	Tellegen, Toon 16
Bessora 41	Jansson, Tove 29	Teller, Janne 54
Blake, Stéphanie.....................10	Jung, Reinhardt 30	Tullet, Hervé 16
Braun, Dieter 22	Kaaberbøl, Lene 30	Turtschaninoff, Maria.....................54
Britt, Fanny 23	Kästner, Erich 30,31	Van Kooij, Rachel 46
Bruna, Dick 10	Kazemi, Nahid.....................13	Van Lieshout, Ted 54
Bsharat, Ahlam.....................42	Könnecke, Ole 13	Velthuijs, Max 17
Chen, Chih-Yuan 10	Lagercrantz, Rose 31	Verne, Jules.....................47
Chotjewitz, David 42	Lagerlöf, Selma.....................31	Vincent, Gabrielle.....................17
Cohen-Scali, Sarah 49	Leray, Marjolaine 14	Walsh, María Elena 40
Collodi, Carlo 23	Lindgren, Astrid 31,32	Wenxuan, Cao 47
Ćopić, Branko.....................11	Magnason, Andri Snær 32	Wolf, Cendrine 36
D'Adamo, Francesco 42	Mankell, Henning 45	Wyss, Johann David.....................48
Dalager, Stig.....................42	Martins, Isabel Minhós 14	Zafón, Carlos Ruiz 48
De Beer, Hans.....................11	Maurois, André.....................33	Zenatti, Valérie 55
De Brunhoff, Jean 11	Melchior, Stéphane.....................45	
De Fombelle, Timothée.....................23,43	Mercier, Johanne 33	
De Saint-Exupéry, Antoine.....................24	Meyer, Kai.....................52	
De Velasco, Stefanie 50	Mizielińska, Aleksandra 33	
De Vigan, Delphine.....................50	Mizieliński, Daniel 33	
Dias, Maria Ana Peixe 24	Modiano, Patrick 34	
Do Rosário, Inês Teixeira 24	Moers, Walter.....................34	
Dragt, Tonke.....................24	Murail, Marie-Aude 53	
Dumas, Alexandre 43	Nesbø, Jo 35	
Ende, Michael 25	Nilsson, Ulf 14,35	
Enzensberger, Hans Magnus 25	Nöstlinger, Christine 35	
Erlbruch, Wolf.....................12	Oesterheld, Héctor Gérman 53	
Feth, Monika 50	Ohlsson, Kristina 35	
Filipovic, Zlata 25	Ohmura, Tomoko 14	
Frank, Anne.....................44	Parr, Maria 36	
Funke, Cornelia 26,44	Pennac, Daniel 36	
Furnari, Eva.....................26	Pfister, Marcus.....................15	
Gaarder, Jostein.....................51	Plichota, Anne 36	
Geda, Fabio.....................44	Preussler, Otfried 37	
Goscinny, René.....................26,27	Prøysen, Alf.....................37	
Greder, Armin.....................27	Pullman, Philip 45	
Grimstad, Lars Joachim.....................27	Roy, Sandrine Dumas.....................15	
Gripari, Pierre.....................28	Salten, Felix.....................37	
Guène, Faïza 51	Salvi, Manuela 53	
Guettier, Bénédicte 12	Sandén, Mårten.....................38	
Hanika, Beate Teresa 51	Satrapi, Marjane.....................45	

Index of Titles

Adventures of Tintin, The 28
Alpha 41
Anton and Piranha 22
Anton Can Do Magic 13
April the Red Goldfish 14
Arcadia Awakens 52
Arthur and the Mystery of the Egg 33
As Red as Blood 54
Asterix the Gaul 26
Bambert's Book of Missing Stories 30
Bambi: A Life in the Woods 37
Bartolomé: The Infanta's Pet 46
Before We Say Goodbye 49
Belle and Sébastien: The Child of the
   Mountains 21
Book of Pearl, The 43
Bridge to the Stars, A 45
Bronze and Sunflower 47
Brothers 54
Brothers Lionheart, The 32
Can You Whistle, Johanna? 15
Cat Who Came in off the Roof, The ... 38
Catherine Certitude 34
Catlantis 39
Code Name: Butterfly 42
Dad with 10 Children, The 12
Daniel Half Human 42
David's Story 42
Day No One Was Angry, The 16
Detective Gordon: The First Case 35
Diary of a Young Girl, The 44
Disappearing Children, The (Prime
   Minister Father and Son) 27
Doctor Proctor's Fart Powder 35
Don't Cross the Line! 14
Duck, Death and the Tulip 12
Elephantasy, An 40
Emil and the Detectives 30
Ernest and Celestine 17
Eternaut, The 53
Eye of the Wolf, The 36
Factory Made Boy, The 35
Fattypuffs and Thinifers 33
Finn Family Moomintroll 29
Flying Classroom, The 31
Frog in Love 17
Fuzz McFlops 26
Girl Detached 53
Glass Children, The 35
Good Little Devil and Other
   Tales, The 28

Grandpa's Guardian Angel 9
Guji-Guji 10
Head of the Saint, The 41
Hedgehog's Home 11
Heidi 39
Hen Who Dreamed She Could
   Fly, The 29
Hot Air 15
House without Mirrors, A 38
Hundred Million Francs, A 22
I Am David 28
In the Sea there are Crocodiles 44
Inkheart 26
Island, The 27
Jane, the Fox and Me 23
Just Like Tomorrow 51
Krabat 37
Learning to Scream 51
Letter for the King, The 24
Line of Fire 41
Line Up, Please! 14
Little Black Fish, The 10
Little Frog 15
Little Polar Bear 11
Little Prince, The 24
Maresi (The Red Abbey Chronicles) 54
Marvellous Fluffy Squishy Itty
   Bitty, The 9
Max 49
Meet at the Ark at Eight 28
Midnight Palace, The 48
Miffy 10
Mr Leon's Paris 9
Mrs Pepperpot to the Rescue and
   Other Stories 37
My Brother Simple 53
My Happy Life 31
Neverending Story, The 25
Nicholas 27
No and Me 50
Northern Lights: The Graphic Novel ... 45
Nothing 54
Number Devil, The 25
Oh, Freedom! 42
Oksa Pollock: The Last Hope 36
Orange House, The 13
Outside: A Guide to Discovering
   Nature 24
Over a Thousand Hills I Walk
   with You 52
Pasta Detectives, The 39

Persepolis: The Story of an Iranian
   Childhood 45
Pinocchio 23
Pippi Longstocking 31
Poo Bum 10
Press Here 16
Rainbow Fish, The 15
Ronia, the Robber's Daughter 32
Sailor Moon 46
Secret of the Blue Glass, The 29
Secrets in the Fire 45
Shola and the Lions 21
Snowman and the Sun, The 16
Sophie's World 51
Story of a Seagull and the Cat Who
   Taught Her to Fly, The 38
Story of Babar, The 11
Story of the Blue Planet, The 32
Story of the Little Mole Who Knew It
   Was None of His Business, The 13
Strawberry Picker, The 50
Struwwelpeter 12
Swiss Family Robinson, The 48
Tales of Hoffmann 52
Thief Lord, The 44
13½ Lives of Captain Bluebear, The ... 34
Three Musketeers, The 43
Tiger Milk 50
Toby Alone 23
Trip to Panama, The 13
Twenty Thousand Leagues
   under the Seas 47
Under Earth, Under Water 33
Vango: Between Sky and Earth 43
Vitello Gets a Yucky Girlfriend 21
Waffle Hearts 36
When I Was a Soldier 55
When We Were Alone in the World 14
Wild Animals of the North 22
Why We Took the Car 52
Wildwitch: Wildfire 30
Wonderful Adventures of
   Nils Holgersson, The 31
Zlata's Diary 25

Index of Translators

Adams, Sarah (see Ardizzone, Sarah)
Aitken, Martin 54
Alexander, Sam 17
Altenberg, Karin 38
Ardizzone, Sarah ....
.... 9,14,15,23,36,41,43,51
Barslund, Charlotte 30
Bartlett, Don 27
Bedrick, Claudia Zoe 9
Bell, Anthea ....
.... 13,17,26,27,30,31,35,37,50,52
Brock, Geoffrey 23
Brownjohn, John 34
Buchanan-Brown, John 22
Bugaeva, Jane 39
Burgess, Linda 10
Butcher, William 47
Calleja, Jen 22
Chace, Tara 35
Chambers, Whittaker 37
Chidgey, Catherine 12,13
Colmer, David 38
Costa, Margaret Jull 21
Crampton, Patricia 32
Crawford, Elizabeth D. 52
Curtis, Howard 44
Curtis, S.D. 11
D'Arcy, Julian Meldon 32
Delargy, Marlaine 35
Denny, Norman 33
Derbyshire, Katy 51
Eaton, Annie 45
Entrekin, Alison 26
Ferris, Blake 45
Flanagan, William 46
Franceschelli, Christopher 16
Garde, Ruth 21
Godwin, William 48
Gordon, Sam 43
Graves, Lucia 48
Greaves, Lucy 24
Greder, Armin 27
Hahn, Daniel 14,33,40,41
Hall, Eileen 30,39
Heim, Michael Henry 25
Helweg, Marianne 37
Hirano, Cathy 14
Hockridge, Derek 26
Hollindale, R.J. 52
Hueston, Penny 49
Hunter, Adriana 53,55

James, J. Alison 15
Jones, Olive 11
Kelly, Lizzie 12
Kim, Chi-Young 29
Kingsland, L.W. 28
Lanning, Rosemary 11
Latsch, Oliver 44
Lewis, Sophie 28
Lloyd-Jones, Antonia 33
Lonsdale-Cooper, Leslie 28
Mackie, Siân 27
Manheim, Ralph 25
Mari Maramoto 46
Marshall, Julia 14,15,31,35
Massotty, Susan 44
McEwen, Alistair 49
McQuinn, Anna 15
Mena, Erica 53
Miller, George 50
Miller, Kane 10
Mitton, Tony 10
Mohr, Tim 50,52
Møller, Paulette 51
Morelli, Christelle 23
Muir, Denise 53
Nagelkerke, Bill 16
Norlen, Paul 31
Norminton, Gregory 21
Nunnally, Tiina 31
Orgel, Doris 42
Osterfelt, Frances 42
Ouriou, Susan 23
Parkinson, Siobhan 46
Peden, Margaret Sayers 38
Pevear, Richard 43
Platt, Alexander 12
Portch, Elizabeth 29
Pribichevich-Zoric, Christina 25
Prime, A.A. 54
Pullman, Philip 45
Puzey, Guy 36
Ragg-Kirby, Helena 28
Rassi, Azita 10,13,16
Ripa, Mattias 45
Roberts, Nancy 42
Robson, Cheryl 42
Rodarmor, William 34
Rose, Sue 36
Salway, Lance 54
Stuksrud, Anne Connie 45
Takemori, Ginny Tapley 29

Tate, Joan 32
Thompson, Laurie 45
Turner, Michael 28
Wang, Helen 47
Watkinson, Laura 24
Williams, Siân 42
Witesman, Owen F. 54
Woods, Katherine 24
Wright, Chantal 22,39